COPE

**Directory of post-16 residential education and training
for young people with special needs**

Eighth edition

ISBN 1 902876 02 4

Published by Lifetime Careers Wiltshire Ltd,
7 Ascot Court, White Horse Business Park,
Trowbridge BA14 0XA

© Lifetime Careers Wiltshire Ltd, 2000.

Cover photograph reproduced with the kind permission of The Treloar Trust, Alton, Hants

Printed by Antony Rowe Ltd

Contents

St Catherine's School

Incorporating Grove Hill Further Education Centre

Grove Hill Further Education Centre offers young people with specific language disorders an integrated educational programme, which blends vocational courses, speech and language therapy and independent living skills within a residential setting. There are 24 places for students aged 16 - 18.

Aims and objectives

- ☐ To improve students' communicative ability
- ☐ strengthen their learning skills,
- ☐ raise their literacy and numeracy competence
- ☐ try out courses at our local college
- ☐ enjoy a variety of work experience and grow in personal and social maturity.

Curriculum structure

A flexible combination of nationally-accredited courses, over a two year period, provides the framework for the delivery of a broad, balanced and relevant curriculum which is individually tailored to meet each student's specific needs

Speech and language therapy

Individual speech and language therapy, group therapy sessions and therapy support within the classroom promote functional communication skills and encourage maximum academic and social progress- Negotiated and agreed courses of therapy, incorporating personal targets, assist the development of responsibility for self-management of any persisting difficulties with comunication.

Pastoral care

Education and therapy programmes are supported by residential independence training. This reinforcement enables students to apply their newly-acquired social language skills.

Grove Road, Ventor. Isle of Wight PO38 1TT   Tel: 01983 852722 Fax: 0198 857219

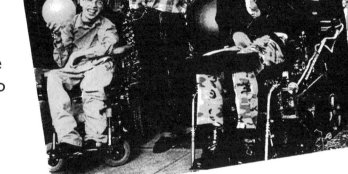

Introduction

This is the eighth edition of COPE. It has been compiled from information received from the many establishments which provide residential, continuing education and training for young people with special educational needs and disabilities. COPE is a quick-reference guide for professionals and carers involved in supporting and advising such young people.

In COPE we have tried to bring together information about a wide range of establishments, run under many different regimes and philosophies. Their approaches to education and training may vary, but they are all devoted to providing support and encouragement to young people with a variety of special needs.

What you will find in COPE

The information about establishments in COPE has been drawn from material gathered from them in late 1999 and early 2000. We have used, as far as possible, the original wording of the replies we received, in order to reflect the flavour and stated aims of the establishments.

- We have tried to include not only establishments which provide formal education, but also those whose goals could be summarised as *preparation and training for adult life*. While we appreciate that many schools offer facilities for their pupils beyond the age of 16, in the context of COPE, our criteria for inclusion are that there should be residential facilities available (at least for weekly boarding) and that applications can be accepted from a wide area. We always welcome details of any establishments that we have missed out.

- Establishments within COPE are indexed by name, geographical area, specialisation in a particular disability and by controlling body.

- The inclusion of an establishment in COPE does not imply a recommendation by us or any judgement of the quality of the education or training provided. We recommend that, if you are investigating training or education for a young person, you should use this book solely as a starting point; it is vital to check details with the establishments themselves. We hope that, in this context, you will find COPE a useful addition to your bookshelf.

Please address comments and suggestions to:

Murray Marshall - *Publications Development Manager*
Lifetime Careers Wiltshire Ltd
7 Ascot Court
White Horse Business Park
Trowbridge BA14 0XA
Email: sales@wiltshire.lifetime-careers.co.uk

Societies Offering Advice on Specific Disabilities

Many of the organisations and societies listed below offer a range of services concerned with assessment, training and employment, as can be seen from entries in COPE. Additional comments are made about some organisations where facilities are known to the authors; however, this is not intended to be a comprehensive coverage of services offered.

Please note that many of the smaller organisations tend to move quite frequently and keeping up with address changes is thus difficult. If you experience problems in contacting the addresses below, check with the Disability Rights Handbook, published annually, which contains a comprehensive list of societies and organisations.

Arthrogryposis

Arthrogryposis Group - 1 The Oaks, Gillingham, Dorset SP8 4SW. Tel: 01747 822655.

Asthma

National Asthma Campaign - Providence House, Providence Place, London N1 0NT. Tel: 020 7226 2260. Fax: 020 7704 0740. Helpline: 0845 701 0203. Website: www.asthma.org.uk

National Asthma Campaign Scotland – 21 Coates Crescent, Edinburgh EH3 7AF Tel: 0131 226 2544. Fax: 0131 226 2401.

Attention deficit

Attention Deficit Hyperactivity Disorder Society – 1a High Street, Dilton Marsh, Westbury BA13 4DL. Tel: 01373 826045. Fax: 01373 825158. Email: gillmead@hotmail.com

Autism/ Asperger's Syndrome

Autism Initiatives - 7 Chesterfield Road, Crosby, Liverpool L23 9XL. Tel: 0151 330 9500. Website: www.autism-initiatives.co.uk/

National Autistic Society/Asperger Syndrome Support Network - 393 City Road, London EC1V 1NE. Tel: 020 7883 2299. Fax: 020 7833 9666. Helpline: 020 7903 3555. Website: www.oneworld.org/autism_uk Email: nas@nas.org.uk

Scottish Society for Autism - SSA headquarters, Hilton House, Alloa Business Park, Whins Road, Alloa FK10 3SA. Tel: 01259 720044. Fax: 01259 720051. Website: www.autism-in-scotland.org.uk Email: autism@autism-in-scotland.org.uk

Society for the Autistically Handicapped - 199-205 Blandford Avenue, Kettering, Northants NN16 9AT. Tel: 01536 523274. Fax: 01536 523274. Website: www.autismuk.com Email: autism@rmplc.co.uk

Blindness and partial sight

National Federation of the Blind - 215 Kirkgate, Wakefield WF1 1JG. Tel: 01924 291 313. Fax: 01924 200 244. Email: mfbuk@globalnet.uk

Partially Sighted Society - 9 Plato Place, 72-74 St Dionis Road, London SW6 4TU. Tel & Fax: 020 7371 289.

Royal National Institute for the Blind - 224 Great Portland Street, London W1N 6AA. Helpline: 0845 7669 999 Website: www.rnib.org.uk Email: helpline@rnib.org.uk

See also Deaf/blind and Retinitis pigmentosa

Brittle bones

The Brittle Bone Society - 30 Guthrie Street, Dundee DD1 5BS. Tel/Min: 01382 204 446. Fax: 013852 206 771. Helpline: 08000 28 24 59. Website: www.brittlebone.org Email: bbs@brittlebone.org

Cerebral palsy	**Capability Scotland** - Rhuemore, 22 Corstophine Road, Edinburgh EH12 6HP. Tel: 0131 313 5510. Fax: 0131 346 1681. Website: www.capability-scotland.org.uk Email: capability@capability-scotland.org.uk
	SCOPE - 12 Park Crescent, London W1N 4EQ. Tel: 020 7636 5020. Website: www.scope.org.uk
Chest and heart	**Stroke Association** - Stroke House, 123-127 Whitecross Street, London EC1Y 8JJ. Tel: 020 7566 0300. Fax: 020 7490 2686. Website: www.stroke.org.uk Email: stroke@stroke.co.uk
Cystic fibrosis	**Cystic Fibrosis Trust** - 11 London Road, Bromley, Kent BR1 1BY. Tel: 020 8464 7211. Fax: 020 8313 0472. Website: www.cftrust.org.uk
Deafness	**Breakthrough** - Deaf Hearing Integration, Birmingham Centre, Alan Geale House, The Close, West Hill Campus, Bristol Road, Selly Oak Colleges, Birmingham B29 6LN. Tel: 0121 472 6447. Fax: 0121 415 2323.
	British Deaf Association - 1-3 Worship Street, London EC2A 2AB. Tel/Min: 020 7588 3520. Min: 020 7288 3529. Fax: 020 7588 3527. Website: www.bda.org.uk Email: info@bda.org.uk
	National Deaf Children's Society - The National Office, 15 Dufferin Street, London EC1Y 8PD. Tel: 020 7250 0123. Fax: 020 7251 5020. Website: www.ndcs.org.uk Email: ndcs@ndcs.org.uk
	Royal Association in aid of Deaf People - Walsingham Road, Colchester, Essex CO2 7BP. Tel: 01206 509509. Fax: 01206 577090. Text: 01206 577090. Website: www.royaldeaf.org.uk/ Email: tom.fenton@royaldeaf.org.uk
	Royal National Institute for Deaf People - 19-23 Featherstone Street, London EC1Y 8SL. Tel: 020 7296 8000. Minicom: 020 7296 8001. Fax: 020 7296 8199. Helpline: 0808 808 0123. Website: www.rnid.org.uk Email: helpline@rnid.org.uk
	Royal National Institute for Deaf People Scotland - 9 Claremont Gardens, Glasgow G37 7LW. Tel: 0141 332 0343. Text: 0141 332 5023. Fax: 0141 331 2640. Website: www.show.scot.nhs.uk/ghl/rnid.htm
Deaf/blind	**SENSE HQ** - (National Deaf/Blind and Rubella Association), 11-13 Clifton Terrace, Finsbury Park, London N4 3SR. Tel: 020 7272 7774. Fax: 020 7272 9648. Website: www.sense.org.uk
Down's Syndrome	**Down's Syndrome Association** - 155 Mitcham Road, London SW17 9PG. Tel: 020 8682 4001.
	The Down's Syndrome Educational Trust - The Sarah Duffon Centre, Belmont Street, Southsea, Hants PO5 1NA. Tel: 023 9282 4261. Fax: 023 9282 4265. Website: www.downsnet.org Email: enquiries@downsnet.org
	Scottish Down's Syndrome Association - 158/160 Balgreen Road, Edinburgh EH11 3AU. Tel: 0131 313 4225. Fax: 0131 313 4285. Website: www.sdsa.org.uk Email: info@sdsa.org.uk
Dyslexia	**Adult Dyslexia Organisation** - 336 Brixton Road, London SW9 7AA. Tel: 020 7924 9559. Fax: 020 7207 7796. Email: dyslexia.hq@dial.pipex.com
	British Dyslexia Association - 98 London Road, Reading, Berks RG1 5AU. Tel: 0118 966 8271. Fax: 0118 935 1927. Administration Tel: 0118 966 2677. Website: www.bda-dyslexia.org.uk Email: info@dyslexia-bda.demon.co.uk

Dyslexia Institute - 133 Gresham Road, Staines, Middlesex TW18 2AJ. Tel: 01784 463935. Head office 01784 463851. Website: www.dyslexia-inst.org.uk Email: info@di-headoffice.freeserve.co.uk

Dyslexia UK - Hickerage, Roxwell Road, Writtle, Essex CM1 3SA. Tel: 01245 420462. Fax: 01245 422975. Website: www.dyslexiauk.com Email: joduring@compuserve.com

Scottish Dyslexia Association – Unit 3, Stirling Business Centre, Wellgreen, Stirling FK8 2DZ. Tel: 01786 446 650. Fax: 01786 471 235. Email: dyslexia.scotland@dial.pipex.com

Eczema

National Eczema Society - 163 Eversholt Street, London NW1 1BU. Tel: 020 7388 4097. Infomation line Tel: 0990 118877. Fax: 020 7388.5882. Website: www.eczema.org.uk Email: eczema@nes.u-net.com

Epilepsy

British Epilepsy Association - New Anstey House, Gate Way Drive, Yeadon, Leeds LS19 7XY. Tel: 0113 210 8800. Fax: 0113 391 0300. Helpline: 0800 800 5050. Website: www.epilepsy.org.uk Email: epilepsy@bea.org.uk

Friedreich's Ataxia

Ataxia - The Stable, Wiggins Yard, Bridge Street, Godalming, Surrey GU7 1HW. Tel: 01483 417 111.

General disability organisations

British Council for Disabled People (BCODP) - Litchurch Plaza, Litchurch Lane, Derby DE24 8AA. Tel: 01332 295 551. Fax: 01332 295 580. Info: 01332 298 288. Min: 01332 295 581. Website: www.bcodp.org.uk Email: bcodp@bcodp.org.uk

DIAL UK (National Association of Disablement Information and Advice Lines) - Park Lodge, St Catherine's Hospital, Tickhill Road, Doncaster DN4 8QN. Tel/Min: 01302 310 123. Fax: 01302 310 404. Website: members.aol.com/dialuk Email: dialuk@aol.com

Disability Action (Northern Ireland) - 2 Annadale Avenue, Belfast BT7 3JH. Tel: 028 9049 1011. Min: 028 9064 5779. Fax: 028 9049 1627. Email: disability.action.hq@cinni.org

Disability Resource Team (DRT) - Office 2, Pelmark House, 11 Amwell End, Ware, Hertfordshire SG12 9HP. Tel/Min: 01920 466 005. Fax: 01920 466 031.

Disability Scotland - Princes House, 5 Shandwick Place, Edinburgh EH2 4RG. Tel/Min: 0131 299 8632. Fax: 0131 229 5168. Email: disability.scotland@virgin.net

Disability Wales/Anabledd Cymrun - Llys Ifor, Crescent Road, Caerphilly, Mid Glamorgan CF83 1XL. Tel/Min: 029 2088 7325. Fax: 029 2088 8702. Email: info@dwac.co.uk

Lead Scotland - Queen Mary College, Clerwood Terrace, Edinburgh EH12 8TS. Tel: 0131 317 3439. Min: 0141 423 5710. Fax: 0131 339 7198. Website: www.cali.co.uk/lead Email: lead.scotland@scet.com

Haemophilia

Haemophilia Society - 3rd Floor, Chesterfield House, 385 Euston Road, London NW1 3AU. Tel: 020 7380 0600. Fax: 020 7380 8220. Helpline: 0800 018 6068. Website: www.haemophilia.org.uk Email: info@haemophilia.org.uk

Learning disability

BILD: British Institute of Learning Disabilities - Wolverhampton Road, Kidderminster, Worcestershire DY10 3PP. Tel: 01562 850 251. Fax: 01562 851 970. Website: www.bild.org.uk Email: bild@bild.demon.co.uk

MENCAP - 123 Golden Lane, London EC1Y 0RT. Tel: 020 7454 0454. Fax: 020 7608 3254.Website: www.mencap.org.uk Operates the 'Pathway' employment scheme for people with learning disabilities, advisory services and a range of training and residential establishments.

ENABLE - 6th floor, 7 Buchanan Street, Glasgow G1 3HL. Tel: 0141 226 4541.

Values Into Action - Oxford House, Derbyshire Street, London E2 6HG. Tel: 020 7729 5436. Fax: 020 7729 7797. Website: www.demon.co.uk/via/b Email: via@btinternet.com

Mental illness

MIND - Granta House, 15-19 Broadway, Stratford, London E15 4BQ. Tel: 020 8519 2122. Fax: 020 8522 1725. Website: www.mind.org.uk Email: contact@mind.org.uk

In Touch Trust - 10 Norman Road, Sale, Cheshire M33 3DF. Tel: 0161 905 2440.

Mental Health Foundation - 21 Cornwall Terrace, London NW1 4QL. Tel: 020 7535 7400. Fax: 020 7535 7474. Website: www.mentalhealth.org.uk Email: mhf@mentalhealth.org.uk

Scottish Association for Mental Health - Cumbrae House, 15 Carlton Court, Glasgow G5 9JP. Tel: 0141 568 700. Fax: 0141 471 235.

Young Minds - 102-108 Clerkenwell Road, London EC1M 5SA. Tel: 020 7336 8445. Fax: 020 7336 8446. Website: www.youngminds.org.uk Email: young.minds@ukonline.co.uk

Multiple sclerosis

Multiple Sclerosis Society - 25 Effie Road, Fulham, London SW6 1EE. Tel: 020 7736 6267. Website: www.mssociety.org.uk

Muscular dystrophy

Muscular Dystrophy Group of Great Britain and N Ireland - 7-11 Prescott Place, Clapham, London SW4 6BS. Tel: 020 7720 8055. Fax: 020 7498 0670. Helpline: 0808 800 8000.

Physical disability

Dyspraxia Foundation – 8 West Alley, Hitchin, Herts SG5 1EG. Tel: 01462 454 986. Fax: 01462 455 052.

RADAR - 12 City Forum, 250 City Road, London EC1V 8AF. Tel: 020 7250 3222. Fax: 020 7250 0212. Minicom: 020 7250 4119. Website: www.radar.org.uk Email: radar@radar.org.uk

The Shaftesbury Society - 16 Kingston Road, London SW19 1JZ. Tel: 020 8239 5555. Fax: 020 8239 5580. Website: www.shaftesburysoc.org.uk/ Email: info@shaftesburysoc.org.uk

Polio

British Polio Fellowship - Ground floor, Unit A, Eagle Office Centre, The Runway, South Ruislip, Middlesex HA4 6SE. Tel: 020 8842 1898.fax: 020 8842 0555. Helpline: 0800 018 556. Email: british.polio@dial.pipex.com

Retinitis pigmentosa

British Retinitis Pigmentosa Society - PO Box 350, Buckingham MK18 5EL. Tel: 01280 860 363. Fax: 01280 860515.

Scoliosis

Scoliosis Association UK - 2 Ivebury Court, 325 Latimer Road, London W10 6RA. Tel: 020 8964 5343.

Speech and language disorders

Association for all Speech Impaired Children (AFASIC) - 347 Central Markets, Smithfield, London EC1A 9NH. Tel: 020 7236 3632/6487.

Spina bifida and hydrocephalus

Association for Spina Bifida and Hydrocephalus – 42 Park Road, Peterborough PE1 2UQ. Tel: 01733 555988. Fax: 01733 555985. Website: www.asbah.demon.co.uk Email: postmaster@asbah.demon.co.uk

Scottish Spina Bifida Association - 190 Queensferry Road, Edinburgh EH4 2BW. Tel: 0131 332 0743. Website: http://ourworld.compuserve.com/homepages/ ssbaha/ Email: 101677.765@compuserve.com

Spinal injuries

Spinal Injuries Association (SIA) - 76 St James's Lane, London N10 3DF. Tel: 020 8444 2121. Fax: 020 8444 3761. Website: www.jgrweb.com/sia
Email: sia@spinal.demon.co.uk

Tuberous sclerosis

Tuberous Sclerosis Association - Little Barnsley Farm, Catshill, Bromsgrove, Worcs B61 0NQ. Tel: 01527 871898.

Other useful organisations

Robinia Group - 6 Charlotte Street, Bath BA1 2NE. Tel: 01225 444596.
Website: www.robinia.co.uk

SKILL - 4th Floor, Chapter House, 18-20 Crucifix Lane, London SE1 3JW.
Tel: 0800 328 5050. Fax: 020 7450 0650. Website: www.skill.org.uk
Email: info@skill.org.uk

Financing of Courses

In the previous section, brief mention was made of the importance of clarifying the nature and source of financial support for individuals who attend the various establishments described in this Compendium. Our intention in this section is to provide some general information on this subject. It is dealt with in more detail in the two Skill publications *Financial Assistance for Students with Disabilities in Further Education* and *Training and Financial Assistance for Students with Disabilities in Higher Education*.

Skill also publishes a number of information leaflets on funding. Contact Skill at the address on p10.

Generally, the costs associated with attending a residential establishment can fall into four categories:

- cost of tuition fees

- cost of accommodation, books, travel, etc.

- maintenance and personal income

- extra costs arising from the disability e.g. special support, costs of integration into an establishment where particular aids and equipment - for example for sensory impairment - are not available.

The sources and level of financial support can vary, depending on a number of factors. These include the type of course (whether it is non-advanced or advanced further education or a certain type of vocational training course) and the type of establishment (for example whether it is a school or a college, whether it comes under the remit of the LEA or the Further Education Funding Council, and whether it is registered with the social services department).

There may be variations in policy from one area to another, and different possible combinations of financial support. This may confuse the student or parent. It is important that advice is sought at an early stage from the named person or key worker, from the establishment the student hopes to attend, or from the agencies described below, most of which publish some explanatory information.

Local authority education department

For students in full-time higher education

The student, or the student's family, has to make a contribution to the university or college, as a share of the tuition costs of the course. **These contributions are means-tested, and the size of the contribution will depend on the income of the student or the student's family**. All students must apply to their LEA for assessment, even if they are required to pay the maximum tuition fee (parents' residual income of around £30,000).

For all students, the funding of living costs is through a loan. *Students apply through their LEA at the same time as the application for support with tuition fees - one application covers tuition fees, student loan and any other supplementary grants, including the Disabled Students' Allowance.* Around three-quarters of the loan is non-means tested. Once the students have graduated, and their income rises above £10,000 per year, they will begin to pay back the loan. The student loan does not take benefits into account as income when calculating the loan pay back.

These arrangements apply to students who live in England, Wales or Northern Ireland and who are studying in the UK. Full details are given in the DfEE guide **Financial Support for Higher Education Students.** Telephone 0800 731 9133 for a free copy.

N.B. At the time of writing, changes to the funding arrangements for full-time higher education in Scotland have been announced. Residents of Scotland who attend a Scottish university will not be expected to pay tuition fees 'up front'. They will repay a set amount (£2000) after their course has ended and they are in employment, with a minimum salary of £10,000 per year. These figures will be subject to change.

Disabled Students' Allowances (DSA)

Disabled Students' Allowances are available to meet course-related costs arising from a disability. These allowances are **not** income-related. Support will be in the form of a grant. From Autumn 2000, disabled students on part-time higher education courses will be able to claim the DSA. Full details of the DSA are available from the awarding authority or Skill.

Access funds

Higher education and further education colleges have Access funds that they can award to any students (not just students with disabilities) in financial difficulties. There is a set amount of money available each year.

The Further Education Funding Councils in England and Wales have a legal duty to make sure that there is sufficient provision for full-time further education for all 16 to 18-year-olds; adequate full-time provision for those over 19; and adequate provision of part-time further education for people of all ages over 16. This means they provide most of the funding for local further education colleges.

In carrying out this duty, the Councils have to pay attention to the needs of students with learning difficulties or disabilities. In Scotland, further education colleges receive their funding from a funding unit at the Scottish Office Education and Industry Department. The Scottish Office has broadly similar duties to the FEFCs in England and Wales. In Northern Ireland, FE colleges are funded by the Local Education and Library Boards.

FE sector colleges

The funding allocated to these colleges should include money to pay for meeting the needs of individual students with learning difficulties or disabilities. It is the responsibility of the colleges themselves to build this additional support funding into their budgets and so into the funding which they receive. Students wishing to study at a local college should apply direct to the college concerned.

Under the Disability Discrimination Act 1995, FE colleges have to produce a statement of their provision for disabled students. If they fail to provide what they say they offer, a student can complain to the FEFC, once they have gone through the college's appeal procedure.

Specialist colleges in England and Wales outside the FE sector

Students whose needs cannot be met in an FE-sector college can apply for funding from the FEFC in England or Wales for a place at a specialist independent college. The Councils can pay for students, whose educational needs cannot be met by a local college, to attend a specialist institution, on a residential basis if necessary. Students on courses at specialist colleges can be funded between the ages of 16 and 25, but not necessarily for all this time. The FEFCs usually fund people on courses for one or two years. It may be possible to have this extended, but it depends on the circumstances. If students are over 19 or on a part-time course, their course must, however, be of a type described in schedule 2 of the Further and Higher Education Act 1992. Broadly speaking, schedule 2 courses are vocational in nature or lead to public examinations, or they prepare students for entry onto such courses. Schedule 2 courses include programmes in independent living and communication skills provided they prepare students for other courses under the schedule.

For each student for whom an FEFC-funded place is sought, local authorities are asked to make a recommendation to the Council. This recommendation includes advice on the student's educational need, supporting evidence, and confirmation that suitable provision is not available at an FE sector college. Details of the application procedure and the criteria which the Council uses in deciding whether to pay for a student to attend a specialist college are available from careers advisers or the Council's nine regional offices in England or the FEFC in Wales. The Council's duty to fund a student at a specialist college outside the sector rests on whether or not sector provision can meet their educational need.

The Funding Councils may expect other agencies to contribute towards the cost of the place, e.g. they may expect the social services department to part-fund it if the placement is for social, as well as educational, reasons.

Government-funded vocational training

Allowances are payable to young people participating in government-funded training schemes. Opportunities are available to young people, and to adults.

Although there are no nationally agreed additional allowances for people with disabilities, trainees may qualify for help with necessary support services or specialist equipment. A lodgings allowance may also be paid in certain circumstances. In addition, trainees may qualify for some of the allowances payable by the Benefits Agency (see below). Allowances are available for disabled adults who may participate in government-funded training or attend courses at various residential colleges described in the Compendium (Queen Elizabeth's, St Loye's etc). Applications should in normal circumstances be made by the Disability Employment Adviser.

The DEA is part of the Employment Service, to help/advise people with disabilities in looking for work. The DEA is based at the local Jobcentre. Information on the full range of employment and training services and schemes can be obtained from the Jobcentre.

Social security benefits

The Benefits Agency (part of the Department of Social Security) offers some benefits specifically for people with disabilities, including Severe Disablement Allowance, Disability Living Allowance, Disability Working Allowance and Incapacity Benefit.

Each of these benefits has different and specific criteria for qualifying, e.g. level/type of disability, National Insurance contributions etc. The local Benefits Agency office can provide more details about all benefits, including other, more general benefits like Income Support. Housing Benefit is available for some people for rent costs. This is paid by the local council. Some benefits have specific rules for students. None of them are intended to pay for things like tuition fees, books and transport to college, but some disabled people may qualify for benefits while studying.

Other sources of financial support

Skill produces a range of leaflets on this subject. Also, the Benefit Enquiry Line for people with disabilities (run by the Benefits Agency) can advise. Tel: 0800 882200. Minicom: 0800 243355.

Various voluntary organisations, educational charities and trusts may also be able to assist with certain costs, though only at a low financial level, and they would not be in a position to offer an alternative source of funding to meet the full costs of attending a residential course if the statutory authorities were unable to assist.

For information on bodies which may make awards, refer to the publications - *The Directory of Grant Making Trusts*, the *Charities Digest*, and *Educational Grants Directory* which should be available for reference in local libraries. Also Skill publishes a list of organisations that fund disabled students.

If you experience difficulties or confusion regarding finance, the local authority key worker or specialist careers adviser should be able to direct any enquiries, and give advice on this whole matter.

Skill's Information Service can offer advice about funding entitlements in further and higher education. It is available for telephone calls on 0800 328 5050 (voice) or 0800 068 2422 (text) between 1.30pm and 4.30pm, Monday to Friday.

Acorn Village

Clacton Road, Mistley, Manningtree, Essex CO11 2NJ
Tel: 01206 394124 Fax: 01206 391216
Chief Executive: Mr R J Ablett
Catchment area: No restrictions   Age range: 19 +
Controlled by: Acorn Village Trust
Fees: Variable according to needs. Rising annually.

Acorn Village is a working village community for people with learning difficulties. The aim is to create employment and educational skills to enable people to live in an environment which best suits their own individual needs. The Village Community offers training towards independent living and residential care.

General description

Five group houses, two independent flats, two single flats at Acorn Village and four houses in the local community with additional work opportunity of an attached tearoom. Village Hall on-site for recreational/social/training and public use by special arrangement. Coffee shop run by villagers and staff at Acorn Village as a work skills training facility. Soft toy workshop, weavery studio, woodwork shop. Sessions include horticulture, sports, swimming, music and movement, art classes, computer studies, educational sessions, drama, professional services of physiotherapist, psychologist and speech therapist by referal to the Health Authority. Full social life encouraged. Any avenues of work outside the Village Community are followed up. Acorn Village Trust has two shops, one nearby in High Street, Manningtree (providing work for those who wish to take part) and another 20 minutes away in Brightlingsea. Acorn Village has fully developed outreach and day services for people in the local community.

Staffing: Acorn has a staff of 110 and employs an NVQ assessor/training co-ordinator.

Residents accepted: Registered for residential and independent living. Mixed sexes. Those with learning difficulties.

Applications/selection: Apply direct to Acorn Village and at the same time notify your social services department of your intentions.

Links with other establishments

Registered with Essex social services department.

Out-of-term contact: Residential, always open.

15

Alderwasley Hall School

Alderwasley, Belper, Derbyshire DE56 2SR
Tel: 01629 822586 Fax: 01629 826661
Email: alderwasleyhallschool@honormead.btinternet.com
Principal: Mr Kiran Hingorani, BSc MEd
Catchment area: Nationwide   Age range: 5-19
Controlled by: Honormead Schools Ltd
Fees per term: boarding: from £9480; day: from £5690
(additional fees for special care)

General description

Aims to realize the full potential of children and young people with special educational needs through the provision of high quality education, therapy and care. Alderwasley Hall's main aim is to maximize the communication competency of its pupils.

Alderwasley Hall School is currently one of the largest specialist schools in the UK for children whose special educational needs arise from their difficulties in speech, language and communication.

Communication deficit is a common basic difficulty for many pupils with learning difficulties and other disorders including the autistic spectrum. Speech and language therapy is therefore an integral part of curriculum delivery at Alderwasley Hall School. The school has its own highly specialized approach to speech and language appropriate to its student population.

Children placed in the school fall within the average range of non verbal abilities.

Staffing: Specialist teachers, student support assistants, speech and language therapists, educational psychologist, occupational therapist. Other school support staff.

Students accepted: Day and residential placements for pupils. Pupils with difficulties in speech, language and communication including some children with a diagnosis of autistic spectrum disorders, Asperger's Syndrome and some who have Attention Deficit and Hyperactivity Disorder.

Courses and facilities

Application/selection: Application through Statement of Special Educational Needs and subject to satisfactory assessment.

- Academic and vocational education.
- Careers guidance and work experience.
- National Curriculum assessment and external accreditation and examinations.
- A wide range of community-based activities.
- Enhanced independence and personal responsibility.
- Spiritual, moral and cultural development.

Links with other establishments

Links with mainstream schools and FE colleges. Callow Park separate facility and part of Alderwasley Hall School and Cavendish House independent living unit in Matlock, Derbyshire. Parents and local authority professionals. Green Laud, FE Centre.

Allington Manor School and Therapeutic Community

Allington Lane, Fair Oaks, Eastleigh, Hampshire SO5 7DE

Tel: 01703 692621

Director: Dr. L F Lowestein MA, DipPsych, PhD

Clinical and Educational Psychologist, Chartered Psychologist

Catchment area: Nationwide   Age range: 10-20

Fees: These vary depending on the needs of children, following a full psycho-diagnostic assessment

Aims to provide a comprehensive educational and psychological treatment centre for young people with special needs, be they emotional or educational. The ultimate aim of the school is to develop each individual to his or her maximum and the objective is not merely to develop the individual but also prepare him/her to live with others in society without coming into conflict. We also provide an important psycho-educational assessment service for local authorities and others.

General description

The Centre provides schooling as well as training and has a classroom block as well as the residential centre. It offers an independent psychological service to schools, parents and families, and to business and industry.

Staffing: Available on the staff are a full-time clinical educational psychologist; teachers; care staff and domestic staff. There is also a consultant psychiatrist who may visit on demand; GP, dentist and optician are also available. All seek to develop the physical, social and emotional life of the individual to its maximum through both individual and group psychological therapy sessions available where appropriate.

Students accepted: Young people who require vocational assessment and guidance and training for work or further education.

Applications/selection: Children can be referred by other psychologists and psychiatrists, and both weekly boarding and day placement as well as residential facilities are available for both male and female youngsters.

Links with other establishments

Sports centre in Eastleigh is available for sporting activities as well as what is available at Allington Manor School and Therapeutic Community, which includes a tennis court, volleyball, football and play areas. Social skills are encouraged and there are links also with educational establishments of further education, technical colleges etc.

Apsley Trust Ltd

Apsley House, 128 Richmond Road, Montpelier, Bristol BS6 5ER
Tel & Fax: 0117 924 3152
Manager: Miss Roxanna Changizi
Controlled by: Apsley Trust Ltd   Age range: 18 +
Fees: On application

Aims to provide a safe and homely environment for adults with learning disabilities aged 18 + in which to support them individually to develop skills that will enhance their quality of life by promoting independence, informed choice, fulfilment and personal growth.

General description

Everyone at Apsley House is expected to remember that we are here to support people with learning disabilities in their home. People with learning disabilities have the same rights as everyone else and must be treated with respect and dignity. They may need help to make choices about their lives, learning new things or practising the skills they have learnt. At Apsley House we believe that everyone has the right to enjoy a healthy lifestyle and to develop their abilities as far as they are able.

Apsley House was opened in 1990 to provide a homely, supportive, and caring environment for adults with learning disabilities that will enhance the quality of their lives, develop their independence skills, and provide them with the ability to make informed choices about their lives.

We are situated in Montpelier near the centre of Bristol close to the Bristol bus station. There is easy access to the local shops and the Broadmead shopping centre, sports centre and swimming pool, parks, the City of Bristol College and many other local amenities.

We are based in a beautiful grade 2 listed building with a large easily accessible self-contained garden boasting a small orchard of fruit trees, and a large vegetable patch growing our own organic vegetables, and a barbecue area.

Each resident has their own bedroom decorated to their own taste, and communal use of the lounge, a large craft room/games room, two kitchens (one of which is used as a training kitchen by the residents), a large dining room, and a laundry room.

Our care package is designed to meet the needs and preferences of the individual in supporting them to achieve their full potential in all areas of their lives.

Banstead Place Brain Injury Rehabilitation Centre

Park Road, Banstead, Surrey SM7 3EE
Tel: 01737 365222 Fax: 01737 359467
Principal: Judith Oliver
Controlled by: Queen Elizabeth's Foundation for Disabled People
Catchment area: Nationwide   Age range: 16-35
Fees: On application - reviewed 31st March. Funding negotiated with local authority education and social services departments, AHA, FEFC and exceptionally from compensation settlements

Aims to provide comprehensive assessment, rehabilitation and placement for young adults with acquired brain injuries.

General description

Part purpose-built centre half a mile from Banstead village. Sutton and Croydon centres easily accessible. Extensive use of local facilities - clubs, pubs etc. Development of personal independence, social skills, practical competence in everyday living are essential parts of students' courses. Structured approach using aids, adaptations and electronic equipment where appropriate geared to individual needs. Single study bedrooms and four independent living units help students acquire and practise the skills of independent living.

Staffing: Principal; social worker; four further education tutors; three occupational therapists and technical instructors; three physiotherapists; two speech therapists; one senior psychologist and one qualified assistant; two art therapists; two workshop instructors; care staff to cover 24-hour period of care support (waking night staff); three recreation staff and one orthoptist.

Students accepted: Banstead Place caters for young adults with acquired brain damage or other neurological disorders. All abilities, but cannot accept severe and uncontrollable behaviour problems or students requiring high levels of medical care. An informal visit is always advisable in the first instance.

Applications/selection: Informal enquiry and visits are encouraged prior to forms of application being obtained from the Principal. Preliminary visits will also be arranged on receipt of application forms, where necessary, to determine appropriateness of provision. Waiting time varies according to urgency - approximately one month at present time. (Entry at any time during the year.)

Courses and facilities

Individual courses, based on a neuropsychological assessment, are geared to identification of needs and development of potential. Most stay about 18 months, others longer or shorter according to progress. Cognitive therapies; further remedial education; independence/mobility training including where possible learning to drive and/or use of public transport; vocational assessment; work experience; social/ leisure activities. Many activities are carried out away from Banstead Place, using local facilities.

Comprehensive range of facilities and equipment not generally available for young disabled people, i.e. independent living assessment and experience. Assessment and training (I.T.). Mobility assessment and driving course available at nearby Mobility Centre, C & G Approved Centre.

Links with other establishments

Students may attend a variety of courses held at local colleges of further education - vocational or recreational activities according to individual needs.

Out-of-term contact: Closure for Christmas holidays only i.e. open approximately 50 weeks per year.

Beannacher Camphill Community

Banchory-Devenick, Aberdeen AB12 5YL
Tel: 01224 869250 Fax: 01224 869250
Catchment area: No restrictions   Age range: 19 to mid 20s
Controlled by: Beannachar Ltd
Fees: Presently £399 a week (residential)

Beannachar is a Camphill Community caring for young adults with special needs.

General description

Beannachar was founded in 1978 and is home to roughly 60 people: our 25 resident students and all co-workers and their children share a common life in a large old house (now two living units) and a new purpose-built house, in a rural setting two miles from the city centre of Aberdeen. The cultural, social and economic needs of each one are catered for as part of the community life. Emphasis is placed on each one looking after the needs of the other, so that mutual help is the basis of our common life. In addition to the work and training opportunities, we also offer a variety of therapies, weekly swimming, dancing, hobby groups, crafts and sports sessions, as well as seasonal activities in drama, painting, music and modelling etc. There is a weekly non-denominational service. Full use is made of the amenities of Aberdeen and its surroundings, and great value is placed on building up and sustaining good relationships between co-workers and the students' families, friends and social workers or care managers. Students are required to take four weeks holiday per year - in the summer and in January.

Staffing: 22 full-time volunteers, all living in, some on training courses, 10 on foundation course.

Students accepted: 25 residential places, 8 day places, mixed sexes, young adults with special needs.

Applications/selections: Please apply Elisabeth Phethean. Tel: 01224 869138.

Courses and facilities

Further education and training opportunities in farm, garden, laundry, pottery, weavery, candle making, herb workshop and kitchens.

Links with other establishments

Links with social work departments and other establishments, both local authority and voluntary.

Out of term contact: Always open.

Beaumont College of Further Education

Slyne Road, Lancaster LA2 6AP
Tel: 01524 64278 Fax: 01524 84689
Principal: Arthur O'Brien
Catchment area: Nationwide   Age range: 16-25
Controlled by: SCOPE
Fees: On application

COPE

Beaumont College exists to provide not just the best quality academic education for its students but all the other experiences, support and sense of achievement necessary to enable our students to become successful adults. We have achieved a National Training Award for the quality of our provision.

General description

Fully equipped and purpose-designed buildings. Conveniently situated within the community of Lancaster, with a wide range of sporting activities utilising College and community resources.

Staffing: Curriculum development manager, student services manager, learning support manager, twelve lecturers, physiotherapist, speech and language therapists, health education co-ordinator, three nurses, care staff.

Students accepted: Students with learning difficulties and disabilities whose FE needs cannot be met within their local community.

Application/selection: Application forms available from the Principal. An informal visit can be arranged any time. This is followed by a three-day assessment period.

Courses and facilities

The College course is normally three years in duration. Students' programmes are based upon a thorough initial assessment and a comprehensive ongoing programme of joint planning and review with the student. The College works in partnership with other colleges of further education and an adult college to provide access to the courses most relevant to each individual student.

Links with other establishments

Extensive links with other colleges of further education.

Beddington Centre

Burton Hill House, Malmesbury, Wiltshire SN16 0EG
Tel: 01666 822685
Principal: P Drake
Catchment area: No restrictions   Age range: 16-19
Controlled by: Shaftesbury Society
Fees: Available on request

The principal aim of the Beddington centre for 16 to19-year-olds is to provide learning experiences which will enable the students to maximise their ability to communicate and interact constructively within the community and, in doing so, gain the greatest autonomy over their lives.

General description

The Beddington Centre is a small friendly setting for students who want to take a lifeskills course, including language and numeracy, that is especially tailored to suit the needs of an individual. The students on the course all have physical and learning disabilities of some kind and benefit from the specialist support that is given, each according to need.

Staffing: The centre is under the direction of its own tutor and ancillary support and enjoys the support of teachers, nurses, care staff, classroom ancillaries, occupational therapists, physiotherapists, speech therapists, consultant paediatrician and orthopaedic surgeon attached to the adjacent school, and a visiting independent careers adviser.

Students accepted: Students all have physical disabilities and learning difficulties of some kind. All students benefit from the individualised timetabling and specialised support available.

Applications/selections: Applications must come via sponsoring LEA. Informal visits welcome. Selection based on day visit and available reports.

Courses and facilities

The Centre enjoys excellent facilities including computers with special needs access, hydrotherapy swimming pool, physiotherapy department, workshop, horticultural unit, students' common room and newly-equipped food technology room with adaptations for disability. Residential as well as day places available. The curriculum options incorporate both in house and external accredited courses:

- STRIVE - Structured Training Resource for Independent and Vocational Education
- RSA - National Skills Profile
- ALL - Acreditation for Life and Living Skills.

Students negotiate modules for their individual programmes of study from the following areas: language and communication, numeracy, ICT, social skills, independent living skills, work and leisure skills, health, safety and mobility, catering, horticulture.

Teaching is through small group work, one-to-one instruction; at the local Centre in the well equipped classrooms; in the local community with structured supervision and in linked modules with local mainstream colleges.

Links with other establishments

The Unit has many links with other establishments. Students regularly visit and integrate with other mainstream schools and FE units as well as day centres and adult placements that cater for people with special needs.

Birtenshaw Hall School

Darwen Road, Bromley Cross, Bolton, Lancs BL7 9AB
Tel: 01204 304230 Fax: 01204 597995
Principal: C D Jamieson
Controlled by: Governing body   Age range: 16-19
Catchment area: Within convenient travelling distance of Bolton
Fees per annum: Day:£18,110 (Severe Disability Supplement £5050); Weekly residential:£27,435 (SDS £5400); Termly residential £42,450 (SDS £9450)

Aims to provide education, preparation and training for adult life for students with physical disabilities and associated learning disorders include those with Profound and Multiple Learning Difficulties (PMLD).

General description

The continuing educational provision at Birtenshaw Hall aims to provide opportunities for disabled young people between the ages of 16 and 19 years, to develop the skills and knowledge needed to make the transition from school to as independent and meaningful an adult life as is possible.

For some young people in special education the move out of school at 16+ can be particularly difficult. The continuing educational provision at Birtenshaw Hall aims to provide an environment in which students are expected to take on more adult responsibilities, and to move on to post-school activities, and yet are operating from within a framework that is structured, supportive and challenging. The school aims:

- to continue the educational process from school towards adulthood through the learning, reinforcement and application of appropriate skills, at an appropriate level
- to further personal, social and emotional development
- to develop and encourage self-reliance, initiative, self-esteem and confidence
- to regard each student as an individual and to develop individualised programmes of continuing education within the residential setting
- to provide some residential experience if required
- to provide for equality of opportunity.

Birtenshaw Hall offers an integrated, student-based approach in which personal programmes are devised to suit individual needs and abilities. Most personal programmes will include daily living and life skills activities including: continuing education skills, work experience, unit accreditation via ASDAN, Youth Award Scheme and AQA Unit Award Scheme.

Staffing: The continuing education provision is staffed by two teachers, with additional qualifications in the education of the disabled, and experienced care staff. The level of care staff support will depend on the individual needs of the students.

Students accepted: All physical disabilities including paraplegia, cerebral palsy, spina bifida, muscular dystrophy, asthma and students with head injuries and PMLD.

Applications/selection: Formal application usually through sponsoring LEA or careers officers. Informal enquiries welcome.

Courses and facilities

The facilities include a kitchen area, teaching accommodation and full residential facilities. Some bathrooms are fitted with specialised equipment. Swimming/hydro therapy pool on site. Fully-accessible transport allows for integration into the community. Experienced and qualified therapists provide occupational therapy, physiotherapy, hydrotherapy and speech and language therapy. The residential Head of Care provides nursing services. Consultant medical cover can be provided by a local GP and there are regular visits from a paediatrician and orthopaedic surgeon. Prior to admission, each student's education and medical needs will be fully discussed at a developmental assessment meeting.

Out-of-term contact: Mr C D Jamieson (Principal), Mrs C A Gannon (Administrator).

Bladon House School

Newton Solney, Burton-on-Trent, Staffordshire DE15 0TA
Tel: 01283 563787 Fax: 01283 510980
Email: blandonhouseschool@honormead.btinternet.com
Principal: Mrs B Murfin
Catchment area: Nationwide   Age Range: 5-19
Controlled by: Honormead Schools Ltd
Fees per term: Boarding - £9480, Day - £5690, 50 Week
Boarding - £11,180 (Additional fees for special care).

Aims to realize the full potential of children and young people with special educational needs through the provision of high quality education, therapy and care.

General description

Bladon House is a leading school for identifing and addressing in an holistic way the primary needs of pupils who have a combination of communication disorders and learning difficulties. In some cases the children may have resulting challenging behaviour.

Staffing: Specialist teachers, student support assistants, speech and language therapists, educational psychologist, occupational therapist. Other school support staff.

Students accepted: Day and residential placements. Students accepted have a combination of communication disorders and learning difficulties, in some cases the child may have resulting challenging behaviour.

Application/selection: Application through Statement of Special Educational Needs and subject to satisfactory assessment.

Courses and facilities

Access to National Curriculum, assessment and external accreditation and examiniations. Academic and vocational education, careers guidance and work experience. Community- and work-based activities. Enhanced independence and personal responsibility, spiritual, moral and cultural development.

Links with other establishments

Links with mainstream schools and FE colleges. Keele University. Other establishments which are part of Bladon House School include Abbey Lodge and Mitchells independent living units and Caldwell Hall, Child Development and Assessment Centre. Parents and local authority professionals. Green Laud, FE Centre and the Grange Vocational Assessment and Training Centre.

Botton Village

Danby, Whitby, North Yorkshire YO21 2NJ
Tel: 01287 660871 Fax: 01287 660888
E-mail: botton@camphill.org.uk
Apply to: Welfare and Admissions Group
Catchment area: Unrestricted   Age range: 21 +
Controlled by: Camphill Village Trust
Funding: Available on request

Aims to provide a working community, education and general care for adults with learning difficulties.

General description

The first Camphill village, based upon the principles of Rudolf Steiner, Botton comprises 28 houses, nine workshops (food centre, bakery, creamery, workshops for glass engraving, doll-making, woodwork, printing, candle-making, weaving), five bio-dynamic farms, over 600 acres, and all the other village facilities such as post office, bookshop, shop, health centre etc. All live in individual houses, co-workers and villagers together. Evening social activities include recreational and educational groups, choir, drama, lectures, films, dancing. Religious services are an integral part of village life, though are optional.

Staffing: Voluntary resident staff living as co-workers in the community, together with their children, form one third of the village population.

Residents accepted: Adults with learning difficulties - very varied ability range, but must be capable and willing to do some form of work. Other disabilities would be considered individually. 80 males, 72 females at present.

Applications/selection: Apply to the Welfare and Admissions Group in Botton village. Waiting period can be several years, depending on urgency.

Courses and facilities

No formal courses - a working community with placements for life, where the finding of one's dignity through work is the underlying therapeutic process. However training is given in the various workshops.

Out-of-term contact: Botton does not close for holidays. Information should be available directly from the village at any time.

Boys & Girls Welfare Society (BGWS)

The BGWS Centre, Schools Hill, Cheadle, Cheshire SK8 1JE
Tel: 0161 283 4848 Fax: 0161 283 4747
Website: www.bgws.org.uk
Email: enquiries@bsws.org.uk
Chief Executive: Mr Andrew F Haines
Age range: 7-19

The Boys' and Girls' Welfare Society (BGWS), the largest children's charity operating exclusively in the North-West of England, has grown from its philanthropic foundation in Manchester in 1870, into a leading provider of child care and educational services, working as it now does with around 20 different local authorities in North-West England and the surrounding areas.

General description

BGWS runs two special schools (for physically disabled, autistic and emotionally disturbed children) and a Further Education College for disabled students.

It runs 15 residential care homes, (providing innovative and differentiated care for disturbed, abused, and unhappy young people), a specialist residential service for disabled young people, and a resource centre for young adults with disabilities.

The Society provides a Family Mediation services in Cheshire, Children's Rights Services in Rochdale and runs the GALRO Panel for Halton, Warrington and Cheshire.

It also provides a comprehensive Fostering and Family Placement Service and runs its own training centre.

BGWS' services are all funded by local authorities through fees and contracts. Voluntary income is small, but increasing through heightening the Society's public profile. Voluntary income is exclusively directed to the development of services for children and young people.

Bridget's Hostel for Students with Disabilities

Tennis Court Road, Cambridge CB2 1QF
Tel: 01223 354312 Fax: 01480 830781
Manager: Mrs Jenny Sandland
Catchment area: Unrestricted   Age range: 16 +
Managed by: The Papworth Trust
Fees: On enquiry

To provide accommodation and 24-hour care for students on higher education or further education courses at Cambridge colleges and to support them in an independent lifestyle. To be a resource for other disabled students living elsewhere in Cambridge, and to support the extension of appropriate facilities and services within colleges themselves.

General description

Seven specially-adapted bedsits on the ground floor of a students' hostel in the centre of Cambridge. There are also common dining room and laundry facilities which are used by all the students in the hostel; and there are specially designed bathrooms and wheelchair-charging facilities. The hostel aims to help, where possible, with academic support such as fetching and carrying books and materials from libraries. Each room has a connection to the Internet.

Staffing: One full-time manager; one senior carer; up to eight paid/part-time carers; one full-time academic liaison officer.

Students accepted: 16+ students attending university or other higher education or further education courses in Cambridge.

Applications/selection: Through the manager of Bridget's for accommodation and through the admissions offices of the colleges concerned for the academic place.

Courses and facilities

Students attend local colleges. The hostel is connected to the University's Grants Information Technology Network.

Links with other establishments

Cambridge University and Anglia Polytechnic University.

Broughton House College

Brant Broughton, Lincoln LN5 0SL
Tel: 01400 272929 Fax: 01400 273438
Head: Mr Bob Noble, Cert Ed, DipEd
Catchment area: Nationwide   Age range: 16-25
Controlled by: The Hesley Group, The Coach House, Hesley
Hall, Tickhill, Doncaster DN11 9HH. Tel: 01302 866906,
Fax: 01302 865473
Fees: On request from the Head.

Broughton House college is a residential college for students with challenging behaviours as a result of autism and/or severe learning difficulties. The aim of all Hesley Group schools and colleges is to enable people with special needs to achieve their full potential. Broughton offers warmth, security, consistency and understanding. The College's philosophy is based on the principles of Gentle Teach, an approach to managing challenging behaviour based on non-aversive positive intervention, as advocated by The Institute of Applied Behaviour Analysis (USA). We seek to understand the behaviour, to identify its function and, by teaching alternative, more appropriate ways of achieving that function, aim to reduce the severity and frequency of the challenging behaviour.

General description

Broughton is a registered Home (1984 Act) and will be seeking FEFC accreditation during the year 2000. The campus is 12 miles from Lincoln and is housed in what was once the Rectory to the magnificent neighbouring church. The house itself is over 200 years old and is well sited in its own extensive grounds, yet close to the local village and its amenities.

Courses and facilities

The students' educational timetables follow a balance of individual programmes to develop personal skills and groups sessions to develop interaction, social skills and tolerance of others. Therapeutic facilities include the Snoezelen for relaxation and counselling, and a multi-sensory room for stimulation and cognitive focusing. Various specialists are on call when required. These include an educational psychologist, clinical psychologist, psychiatrist, speech and language therapist, occupational therapist and physiotherapist.

Students accepted: 23 residential placements.

Referrals and admissions: A student will be considered for a placement once an official request us received from the LEA, Social Services, or other referring agency. However, parents are encouraged to visit on an informal basis so that they can meet staff and students.

Parent Partnership: The college is a strong advocate of teamwork between all agencies, and especially the student's parents and family. Contact with parents is maintained throughout the student's life at Broughton through phone calls, home visits and visits by parents to their son or daughter.

Links with the community: this is an essential part of the daily life of our students, and includes leisure pursuits - skating, horse riding, swimming and bowling - and social training, when they will visit local shops, learn to use public transport and other amenities. Many of our students also access courses at the local FE college.

Work experience: Broughton aims to provide all its students with a variety of learning experiences which are relevant to their own individual needs. Students will take part in a choice of work-based activities as preparation for attending further work experience projects with approved centres.

Bryn Melyn

Llandderfel, Bala, Gwynedd LL23 7RA
Tel: 01678 530330 Fax: 01678 530460
Website: www.brynmelyn.demon.co.uk
Email: c.price@brynmelyn.demon.co.uk
Catchment area: Nationwide   Age range: 12 +
Controlled by: Independent; registered with Gwynedd County Council
Fees: £3590 per week + VAT

Aims to prepare vulnerable and difficult young people for self-reliant living situations or transition into appropriate adult treatment situations. Emphasis is placed on life and social skills training, work experience. Intensive therapeutic work on a 1:1 basis. Additional specialised inputs as appropriate.

For further information

Please contact: Mrs Janet Rich

Brochure; therapy practice and programmes; statement of purpose and function; copy of latest registration and inspection report, all available on request.

Applications/selection: By admissions process (available on request).

Students accepted: Both sexes. Abused young people and young offenders.

Links with other establishments

Local schools and tertiary colleges. Extensive range of outdoor activity centre and inter-agency contact.

The Bryn Melyn Group also operates Crisis Intervention Services for young people under the 'Mentors' name and specialised services for sex offenders and young people with sexually aggressive behaviour.

Camelia Botnar Foundation

Maplehurst Road, Cowfold, West Sussex RH13 8DQ
Tel: 01403 864556
Catchment area: Nationwide   Age range: 16-19
Controlled by: Board of Trustees
Fees: None

Aims to help young people who are deprived, through no fault of their own, due to domestic or financial circumstances. To provide both employment and accommodation for them, while paying them a wage.

General description

The Foundation is a self-supporting charity based on a 500-acre country estate. All the enterprises are run as closely as possible along normal commercial lines. The trainees are paid a commercial wage and make a contribution towards their board and lodging. The objective is that, after a spell of work experience (up to two years) and living as one family at the Foundation, they will be ready to hold their own as mature individuals in the 'outside world'.

Staffing: House parents and department management.

Students accepted: Students of both sexes. Regret no facilities for mental or physical problems.

Applications/selection: Written application with brief social history, followed by interview.

Courses and facilities

Areas of employment: Building, carpentry, catering, metalwork, painting and decorating, horticulture, landscape gardening.

Links with other establishments

All trainees are encouraged to take appropriate courses at local colleges on day release.

Out-of-term contact: All contact via office at the Foundation, open all the year, normal office hours.

Camphill Blair Drummond

Blair Drummond House, Cuthil Brae, By Stirling FK9 4UT
Tel: 01786 841573
Principal: The Senior Co-worker Group
Catchment area: No restrictions   Age range: 16-29
Controlled by: Council of Management Camphill Blair Drummond Trust Ltd
Fees: £18,690 p.a. for a 42-week year

Aims to provide further education and craft training. The broad aim is to enable individuals to improve basic scholastic and manual skills, and mature into stable adults who have learnt to work to the best of their ability. Social integration and community living are very important.

General description

Camphill Blair Drummond is one of the therapeutic communities of the Camphill Movement, situated six miles from Stirling, two miles from Doune. There are six family group houses on a 17-acre plot of land. Four of the house units are within the walls of a large baronial-type Scottish mansion. Students use local facilities as and where appropriate e.g. shops, swimming pool, horseriding, etc.

Co-workers: All co-workers live in the family units together with the residents. Camphill offers its own extensive training programmes and all co-workers receive ongoing weekly training. Medical care, paramedical care, etc is provided by local professionals as needed.

Students accepted: Prefer to admit at age 16. Most people leave in their mid to late 20s. 40 trainees, both sexes, mixed disabilities, though primarily those with learning difficulties. Can cater for some individuals with additional physical, social or mental illness/disabilities.

Applications/selection: Applications in writing are sent to the admissions committee. As full reports as possible required, particularly of early development. Parents, applicant and relevant professionals are invited for interview. Application and placement must be supported by education or social work departments. A trial period of six weeks is offered, this can be extended if necessary. Waiting time is very varied - but application in good time is advisable. All residents go through a yearly review procedure.

Links with other establishments

Camphill Blair Drummond has many and varied links with other establishments. Locally, mainly with riding and swimming for the disabled. If appropriate, with local colleges, employers, psychiatric and social work services, etc. On a more national level, with other Camphill and Steiner organisations, as well as other bodies.

Out-of-term contact: There is always someone at Camphill Blair Drummond during holiday periods.

Camphill Rudolf Steiner Schools

Murtle Estate, Bieldside, Aberdeen, Scotland AB15 9EP
Tel: 01224 867935 Fax: 01224 868420
Website: www.camphillscotland.org.uk
Email: office@crss.org.uk
Principal: Joint Co-ordinators Group
Age Range: 3-24
Status: Independent (Scotland) DfEE Registered
Fees: £22,600 - £45,200 per annum

Camphill's work is born out of Rudolf Steiner's Philosophy and founded by Dr Karl Konig. By co-workers living with the pupils in their care without wages, a unique rapport is established between co-workers, pupils and co-workers' own children. House life and school life have their structure and rhythm giving security. Through teachers, therapists, etc. also sharing in house life, progress and concerns can be compared continuously and brought quickly to the appropriate formal meeting. Aiming to understand a child and his/her individual experiences, we would hope to lead and accompany him/her into a fulfilling adulthood. Camphill caters for children with a wide range of disabilities; each can make a real contribution and achieve dignity.

General description

The schools comprise 125 acres on Lower Deeside; local shops and direct bus route to Aberdeen. Farmed organically, the Estates supply the houses with fresh produce. A rich cultural environment replaces television, with children, adults and visiting performers involved in plays, pageants, concerts etc. culminating each term with community-based celebration of the Christian festivals.

Staff qualification and selection: Selection is via the Co-worker Committee and complies with guidelines laid down by the Children Act. Co-workers either participate in a one-year Foundation course or a four-year BA in Curative Education, in partnership with Northern College, Aberdeen and accredited by the Open University.

Established: 1940

Number on Roll: 118

Type of School: Mixed. Full/weekly boarding and day.

Teaching Staff: 40; Residential Care Staff: 30; Special Needs Support Staff: 80

Length of School Year: 40 weeks (4 term year).
Scottish Education Department School Code: 528 1040

Specialist facilities: Camphill has a unique community-based lifestyle and has developed a full range of individual and group therapies. Based on child development, the Waldorf curriculum (classroom) has shown its therapeutic value in working with developmental delay. A Further Education programme comprises school, work projects, crafts and work experience (currently part of the Accreditation Programme of the National Autistic society).

Support services provided: NHS homeopathic medical practice, internal 'clinics' and 'college meetings', statutory reviews and regular visits of consultants. As pupils reach 16, future placements are discussed with family and LEA, and may or may not be within a Camphill setting. The Camphill Association in GB includes the Camphill Counselling Service.

Home school links: Regular contact is encouraged. Each child's annual report is written primarily for the parents. A yearly parents' weekend.

Catherine House

> Catherine Hill, Frome, Somerset BA11 1BY
> Tel: 01373 463172
> Principal: Mr Andrew Chiffers
> Age range: 16-19
> Catchment area: Nationwide
> Controlled by: Farleigh Schools Ltd
> Fees: available on request

Catherine House is a new residential specialist further education college, opening in September 2000, for students with Asperger's Syndrome.

General description

Catherine House will offer a 24-hour curriculum, including a communication and social skills programme in the community. The curriculum will offer structured independence training. Students will follow individual academic programmes, according to their needs, and will be prepared for higher education, training or employment. Programmes are likely to last for at least two years, exact duration will be agreed according to individual need.

Students will have access to specialist teachers, mainstream lecturers, educational psychologist, speech and language therapist and external consultants.

Accommodation will be provided in Catherine Hill House; opportunities for independent living will be developed.

Students accepted: male and female; there will be up to 10 places.

Links with other establishments

Links are being developed with Trowbridge College and with schools in the area.

Cherry Orchards Camphill Community

Canford Lane, Westbury-on-Trym, Bristol BS9 3PE
Tel: 0117 950 3183 Fax: 0117 959 3665
Website:www.camphill.org.uk
Chairman: T Koeller
Catchment area: Nationwide   Age range: 20-45 approx
Controlled by: Independent; member of Association of Camphill Communities
Fees: On application

Cherry Orchards aims to be an integrated therapeutic community.

General description

Cherry Orchards is on 17 acres of green belt with fields, a little valley with a stream, a vegetable garden and woodland. Residents and co-workers (staff) live integrated with one another and share the burdens and pleasures of domestic life. There are three houses which offer a safe, residential therapeutic environment with many therapeutic activities including art, basketry, weavery, candle-making, gardening etc.

Staffing: All staff work as full-time voluntary workers and 12 are residential.

Residents accepted: Young adults who want to recover from mental health difficulties. Our residents come from all over Britain, and are between approximately 20 and 45 years old. There are up to 15 places. Mixed sex.

Applications/selection: On request a questionnaire will be sent out. Then an interview can follow. Placement is offered when a vacancy occurs - could be immediately or after waiting for several months.

Courses and facilities

Everyone is included in working activities, within which basic skills are taught as part of the work process; always the emphasis is on the meaningfulness of any action. Trainees spend two thirds of the day in the garden and workshops, and one third on classroom education (a variety of subjects are offered) and artistic activities (including painting, modelling, drawing and craftwork). Adults work alongside the staff and are led to see their work as fulfilling a need in the community. Residents who become able are encouraged to find employment and to grow towards independence.

Links with other establishments

Individual links can be established according to need. Bristol offers unlimited possibilities for further development. Cherry Orchards could be the base for this.

Cintre Community

54 St John's Road, Clifton, Bristol BS8 2HG
Tel: 0117 973 8546 Fax: 0117 923 9979
Contact: Catherine Twine
Catchment area: No restrictions   Age range: 16-35
Controlled by: Independent Charity
Fees: £673.40 per week - all day care included. DSS contribute approx. £237 of this

Cintre's aim is to assist residents in taking individual steps towards managing their own lives in a more independent manner. This may result in full or semi-independence.

General description

Cintre has eight key features:

- guidance and support of a key worker
- individual care plans
- work experience and training
- community living
- environmental consciousness
- provision and support of leisure activities
- ideal residential setting
- transitional house - Penmaen.

Staffing: Two members of staff are on duty at all times, plus day care staff.

Client Group: Those with challenging behaviour and learning difficulties.

Applications: Initial visit and interview, then trial period of mutual assessment.

Day Care: Cintre provides day care in:

- arts & crafts
- organic gardening & farming
- home economics
- woodwork.

Long Arm Care: Cintre offers long arm care to individuals that have moved to independent housing but need support, guidance and a safe, social environment.

Links with other establishments

Cintre community has a second wardened-only house, Penmaen, Alexandra Park, Redland, Bristol, BS6 6QB. Cintre works closely with City of Bristol College and other learning and social organisations.

Harbour House is a third unit which has the same aims as Cintre House. It is semi-isolated and offers great scope for organic gardening, animal care as well as the same features as Cintre House.

Opening times: Cintre is open all year round.

COPE

Coleg Elidyr

Rhandirmyn, Llandovery Carmarthenshire SA20 0NL
Tel: 01550 760400 Fax: 01550 760331
Website: www.camphill.org.uk
Principal: Thomas B Koeller
Age range: 16 +
Catchment area: Unrestricted
Fees: £18,500 per annum 99/00 (payable three termly)
Reviewed each August

Aims to educate and train young people with learning difficulties, give them stimulation and help to complete their search for identity, develop their potential, to work towards vocational skills, gain competence in social skills and thereby find enough confidence to meet society as people in their own right.

General description

A Camphill Community based on the principles of Rudolf Steiner with a strong interdenominational Christian background. About 65 students together with staff and their families live in 11 houses on a 200-acre farm providing a labour intensive farm training, including 30 acres woodland, fruit/vegetable gardens and orchards; classrooms; workshops and sports facilities. A further three houses for 21 'apprentices' plus staff and their families, a working farm and substantial market gardens are located at Glasallt Fawr, a 150-acre site near Llangadog. In Llangadog village there are two houses for a further 10 young people and extensive workshops with the possibility to integrate into the locality as a stepping stone towards returning to their own community as is appropriate.

Staffing: Approximately 45 full-time staff, living in. Plus additional full-time and part-time teachers, two nurses, local GPs. Help of local psychiatrists, psychologist, chiropodist and speech therapist where applicable.

Students accepted: Male and female, a range of disability but cannot accept severely physically disabled nor youngsters with severe challenging behaviour.

Applications/selection: Application forms available from the college. Interviews and trial periods to be arranged.

Courses and facilities

Three year non-advanced course of further education and training for approximately 16 to 19 age group. Includes project lessons in general subjects, support for key skills, art, eurhythmy, folk dancing, music, speech lessons. Craft activities in small groups including weaving, woodwork, candle-making and basket-making. Wide variety of work experience: farming (dairy, sheep, pigs), gardening and estate activities, shop-keeping, preserving, cooking and baking, laundry/domestic work, guest house management.

Vocational apprenticeship: some students stay on for a further two years from 19. Each apprenticeship has a curriculum to include vocational and independent living skills but individuals work at their own speed.

NPTC courses in agriculture, horticulutre, IT, independent living skills. Open college courses in weaving, woodwork, care, catering and pottery. LCCI: V.A.C. in retail; Wordpower; Numberpower.

Links with other establishments

These include Llandovery college, CCTA (Carmarthen College of Technology and Art).

Out-of-term contact: There is always a small staff at the college

Corseford School

Milliken Park, Howwood Road, Kilbarchan,
Renfrewshire PA10 2NT
Tel: 01505 702141 Fax: 01505 702445
Website: www.capability-scotland.org.uk
Email: capability@capability-scotland.org.uk
Principal: Mrs M Boyle
Catchment area: The whole of Scotland   Age range: 0 to 19
Controlled by: Capability Scotland
Fees: £439.80 per week for resident children; £336.61per
week for day children

Aims to provide for each pupil an individual programme of education, therapies and care, appropriate to his or her needs. To promote maximum educational, physical and social developments. To provide support for the families by the availability of staff to give advice and encourage parental cooperation and involvement.

General description

The school is situated on the outskirts of Johnstone in Renfrewshire and accommodation within the building, apart from resident staff quarters, is all at ground level and access facilities are excellent. The building is 'H' shaped with residential accommodation in the block facing the main road and with classrooms and therapy departments at the rear.

Staffing: The number of staff in direct contact with the children is 74, with a full-time equivalent of 56. Additionally, we have a support staff of 30, full-time equivalent of 23.29 which gives a total of 104 members of staff, a full-time equivalent of 80.99 and an overall pupil : staff ratio of 1:1.72.

Students accepted: Students accepted with cerebral palsy or with similar needs and with the potential to follow a curriculum which is broadly similar to that of mainstream schools.

Applications/selection: By referral from the education authority to the Principal in the first instance.

Courses and facilities

- Early Education service which is a self-referral, two-four times weekly part-time service for parents, usually mothers, and their pre-school children.

- The management approach to our pupils is eclectic, generally combining the best features of Bobath handling and conductive education.

- Post-16 Unit.

- The school is a national resource and receives some 350-400 visitors, with a professional interest in cerebral palsy, annually. In addition, courses are held, usually one-day courses, for staff working with clients with physical impairments.

Links with other establishments

Various schools and colleges and adult establishments throughout Scotland, also other Capability Scotland establishments.

Cottage & Rural Enterprises Ltd (CARE)

Various locations

Central Office: 9 Weir Road, Kibworth, Leicester LE8 0LQ.

Tel: 0116 279 3225 Fax: 0116 279 6384

Email: carecentral@btinternet.com

Catchment area: National

Controlled by: Cottage & Rural Enterprises Ltd

Fees: The cost of caring is met by DSS benefits and Social Services contributions.

General description

CARE is a national voluntary organisation providing a purposeful and enjoyable lifestyle for men and women with learning disabilities in residential communities in England. Each community provides a variety of useful productive workshop activity, and residents have their own single bed sitting room with own washing facilities in cottages. These cottages have their own staff who are supervised by the manager of the community.

Referral: Self or professional to nearest CARE community or Central Office.

Contact: The Secretary.

The Croft Community

Gawain House, 56 Welham Road, Norton, Malton, North Yorkshire YO17 9DP
Tel & Fax: 01653 697197
Email: andy@croftcvt.demon.co.uk
Website: camphill.org.uk
Catchment area: Nationwide   Age range: 19-60+
Controlled by: Camphill Village Trust
Fees: On application

Aims to assist adults with learning difficulties towards independence and integration within the community by providing a home, work, further education and general care.

General description

A working community located in small friendly market town. Good links with local community. Residents attend churches and evening classes. Music classes are run by local friends. Variety of indoor and outdoor activities, and has six houses within the local community.

Staffing: 16 co-workers.

Residents accepted: Each case considered individually - no automatic exclusions. Wide ability range. 16 males, 15 females at present.

Applications/selection: Apply to Andy Paton at the address below. After interview, a two-week trial working holiday is offered, followed by a pause for reflection. Waiting period approximately one year.

Courses and facilities

There is a working community with activities offered in the garden bookshop/cafe, weavery, paper-making, woodwork, cooking and housework. Some adult education is carried out in the evenings, and there is a rich and varied cultural life including drama, eurhythmy, dance, study groups, and celebration of Christian festivals. Possibility of open employment outside the Community.

Links with other establishments

Evening classes are attended locally. Some people attend local college one day a week.

Out-of-term contact: Andy Paton - The Croft Community, Gawain House, 56 Welham Road, Norton, N. Yorkshire YO17 9DP. Tel: 01653 694197; Ian Parker - The Croft, Old Malton Tel: 01653 694323; Clare Belbin - Greengate House. Tel: 01653 697192.

Dame Hannah Rogers School

Woodland Road, Ivybridge, Devon PL21 9HQ.
Tel & Fax: 01752 892461
Email: fedept@lineone.co.uk
Principal: Mr W R Evans
Catchment area: Nationwide/International   Age range: 16-19
Controlled by: Independent trust and management committee
Fees: Individually assessed according to needs of the student

Aims to prepare students for adulthood, encouraging self dependence and realistic independence to provide a basis on which to build a full and satisfying life. To provide a continuing general education in basic skills and a life skills training programme which will enable our students to develop to their full potential for independent living.

General description

Site is a purpose built suite of classrooms with level access from five residential training bungalows, each housing up to five students. Access to the main school building and swimming pool is via the internal lift, or external pathways. Links with the local community are maintained, through youth clubs, Link up club, leisure centre and churches.

Staffing: Care ratio 2:5; three FTE teachers; seven classroom assistants. Integrated speech and language therapy and physiotherapy programmes for all students. 24-hour nursing.

Students accepted: Neurologically and physically challenged with associated learning difficulties. DHRS is a centre of excellence for the development of AAC (Alternative and Augmentative Communication) for students with little or no speech.

Applications/selection: To Principal. Informal visits are welcome. Family invited to interview, currently a two-day procedure - accommodation may be available at the school. Decision as to the applicability of the course to meet the student's needs, made within five days.

Courses and facilities

External examinations may be offered in conjunction with the local community college. Communication and independence training, AAC curriculum accredited through City & Guilds. General education and life skills training in conjunction with ASDAN (Award Scheme Development and Accreditation Network) modules where appropriate. Waking hours curriculum approach ensures that skills can be consolidated throughout the extended day.

Links with other establishments

Ivybridge Community College, local residential homes and day centres as appropriate to the needs of the students and their courses.

David Lewis Organisation

Mill Lane, Warford, Nr Alderley Edge, Cheshire SK9 7UD
Tel: 01565 640000 Fax: 01565 640100
Age Range: School 5-19, College 19 +
Catchment area: No restrictions
Fees: Variable according to needs

General description

The David Lewis School is a non-maintained residential and day special school for 75 students who have epilepsy and associated learning difficulties. The school is part of the largest multi-disciplinary centre for children and adults with epilepsy in the United Kingdom. Students have access to a range of specialist services including: consultants in epilepsy, trained nursing and teaching staff, educational psychologists, speech and language therapists, physiotherapists, dentist, music therapy and hydrotherapy.

Courses and facilities

The post-16 curriculum provides for the development of core skills and a range of pre-vocational courses. Strong emphasis is placed on skills for life and the Centre offers a range of externally accredited courses.

The post-16 unit offers a wide range of work experience placements both on and off Centre.

In the residential accommodation, students are responsible for tasks involved in the day-to-day running of the house with an emphasis on preparation for independence and transition to adulthood. The houses have a structured programme of activities durng the evening and at weekends appropriate to the individual students's needs.

Deafway

Brockholes Brow, Preston, Lancs PR2 5AL.
Tel: 01772 796461 Fax: 01772 654439
Director: David Hynes
Age range: 18 +
Controlled by: Charitable organisation

Working to provide equality of access and opportunity for deaf people.

General description

Deafway is a registered charity providing a wide range of services including: residential rehabilitation, community work, sports, social and recreational facilities, and the Royal Cross Primary School for Deaf Children.

Students accepted: Deaf people who require care, rehabilitation, or independent living skills training.

Applications/selection: Referrals can be made by local authorities, probation or health authorities in respect of individuals. Following initial assessment, appropriate time-limited care plans or rehabilitation programmes are negotiated.

Courses and facilities

The areas of activity presently being undertaken are:

- educational and technological opportunities
- employment training opportunities
- individual rehabilitation programmes
- individual packages of care
- community support work.

Delrow College

Hilfield Lane, Aldenham, Watford WD2 8DJ
Tel: 01923 856006 Fax: 01923 858035
Website: www.camphill.org.uk
Email: email@delrow.newnet.co.uk
Catchment area: Unrestricted   Age range: 19-60
Controlled by: Camphill Village Trust

Aims to provide assessment, further education and practical help for people with learning difficulties with the intention of rehabilitating them towards life in one of the Camphill Villages or open employment, according to their individual capabilities.

General description

Large house standing in 11 acres of grounds. Buildings are still being developed. Begun in 1963 as an assessment centre, Delrow is now a residential college for rehabilitation and further education. The new college and three new houses have been built. Practical work includes crafts, gardening, kitchen and housework. Wooden and soft toys are made for sale to shops and the public. Over 30 former residents now live and work in the locality and maintain contact with Delrow.

Staffing: Delrow is run on a sharing basis as a community, with no wages being paid.

Students accepted: Those with learning difficulties, mentally disturbed. 60 people, mixed sex.

Applications/selection: Apply to the college.

Courses and facilities

Periods of stay vary from one weekend to several years. As well as lectures and discussion groups on a wide range of subjects, there are courses in speech, movement and music therapy, choral singing and drama. Remedial education and craft training are also part of the college facilities.

Links with other establishments

Member of the Association of Camphill Communities.

Derby College for Deaf People

Ashbourne Road, Derby DE22 3BH

Tel: 01332 297550 (voice) Fax/Text: 01332 206642

Principal: Brenda Mullen

Catchment area: Unrestricted   Age range: 16-25

Aims to provide deaf young people with access to the range of educational opportunities, on and off campus, available to all young people to enable them to develop their own identity and self-confidence and gain esteem from a supportive community of peers and staff, and to assist them to become more independent and self reliant in their social and emotional development.

General description

Derby College for Deaf People is an independent, residential college for deaf and hearing impaired young people. Our students study at local mainstream colleges, which gives them access to a full range of educational opportunities open to everyone. They receive communication and language support, individual tutorial programme, independent living skills, pastoral and social support. Speech and language therapy and sign language tuition are available. Access to a Deaf Counsellor.

Students accepted: Deaf and hearing-impaired young people in the ability range from those with learning difficulties to degree potential.

Applications/selection: Application forms from the college. Interviews and assessments as appropriate.

Courses and facilities

Student support: Support in lectures which is designed to meet specific and changing language needs exactly, whether it be BSL, SSE, note-taking or lip-speaking. We also arrange awareness training for mainstream college lecturers and students.

Our evening Tutorial Programme offers:

- Small group tutorials for GCSE English and maths, Wordpower and Numberpower
- one-to-one tutorials to help them with their coursework
- courses in communication strategies and CACDP British Sign Language
- specific short courses for study skills, job seeking and applications to higher education.

Mainstream courses: All students who come to DCDP have access to nationally recognised qualifications; GNVQ; NVQ; GCSE and A level.

Pre-vocational courses: Vocational Credit Programme - this one or two year programme is taught together with a local mainstream college. It gives students the chance to explore several vocational subjects, as well as giving them intensive basic skills and lifeskills tuition from qualified Teachers of the Deaf. All basic skills and lifeskills programmes are assessed through nationally recognised programmes and qualifications including:

- City & Guilds Wordpower and Numberpower
- AEB numeracy and literacy
- Open college certificate in study skills
- ASDAN FE Award (lifeskills).

Access to further education: This course is designed for students who are not ready to access the local mainstream college, and focuses on developing an individual programme that will meet their educational and personal needs. The students will follow a basic skills curriculum, including literacy, numeracy, communication, computer and independence skills. They will be based in Derby College for Deaf People and will access local FE colleges for individual or group vocational courses.

Derwen College

Oswestry, Shropshire SY11 3JA
Tel: 01691 661234 Fax: 01691 670714
E mail: derwen@enterprise.net
Director: D J Kendall BEng, FCA, MEd
Catchment area: Nationwide   Age range: 16 +
Controlled by: Independent charity with a Board of Governors
Fees: £18,197 per annum (1999/2000)

COPE

Aims to promote the vocational, educational and personal development of young people with a wide range of learning difficulties and disabilities. To provide further education in its broadest sense leading to a maximum degree of independence.

General description

The college is inspected by the Further Education Funding Council and Shropshire Social Services. Set in fifty acres of parkland, the campus has been designed specifically for the diverse needs of the students. The single storey accommodation is of the highest quality and offers students progression from residences with a high level of support to living independently in bungalows within the community. There are impressive sports facilities, including an indoor heated swimming pool and a large multi-purpose sports hall. The infrastructure of the college provides appropriate levels of support so that each student has the chance to develop a set of life skills objectives as part of the total education programme.

The modern medical centre is staffed day and night by qualified nursing personnel, who provide the medical care with the college doctor. Physiotherapy and speech therapy are available and each student has a personal counsellor, with referral to a clinical psychologist if required.

Students accepted: Moderate or severe learning difficulties, with or without a physical disability.

Applications/selection: Prospective students and parents arrange to visit the college, to include a short assessment and a preview of each vocational department, initiating the application process. An initial report is prepared by the end of the visit and the student and parents are then able to decide whether to apply for funding, with the support and guidance of the careers service.

Courses and facilities

Assessment: One term, termly intake

Vocational courses: usually three years (37 weeks a year in residence)

- catering
- horticulture
- hospitality and housekeeping
- office
- practical skills
- retail
- fabrics.

All students have access to National Vocational Qualifications (NVQs).

Out-of-term contact: Mr D J Kendall, Director.

Dilston College

Part of the MENCAP National College Residential and Day FE College, Corbridge, Northumberland NE45 5RJ
Tel: 01434 632692 Fax: 01434 633721
Principal: J A Jameson BA, PGCE
Catchment area: Nationwide for residential students
Controlled by: MENCAP   Age range: 16-25
Fees: Usually within range: Residential - £19,600-£37,000; day - £10,200-£26,200; as per FEFC Funding Matrix. Further details on request

The aim of the college is to support young people with a learning disability in the progression and transition to adult life. It provides them with a range of opportunities, experiences and skills which will be of value to them in the future and will provide access to full community participation as adults. Planned courses and educational support, monitoring and review of progress, and the recording and measuring of outcomes and achievements are essential elements of each individual's learning programme.

General description

Established in 1971, Dilston College is close to both Corbridge and the pleasant market town of Hexham and, with Newcastle within easy reach, there are good rail and road links to all parts of the country. Accommodation is either in single or twin-bedded rooms, in flats, cottages and houses.

Staffing: 60 staff - educational, administrative, care and ancillary.

Students accepted: 50 residential and a number of day students, male and female. Moderate to severe range of learning disability.

Applications/selection: Informal visit. Application form and school and other reports, assessment visit (five days for residential applicants). Application then usually to FEFC with local authority support for funding. Advisable to start application procedure at least one year in advance.

Courses and facilities

Access and achievement: All students follow the Extended Curriculum within an Inclusive Learning model. This provides access to NVQ level 1 in several vocational areas, and a number of other nationally- accredited qualifications (City and Guilds, London Chamber of Commerce and Industry, National Proficiency Tests Council). Basic Food Hygiene Certificate, RSA CLAIT.

The Dilston Curriculum: The Extended Curriculum covers the following areas:

- daily living skills
- social skills
- vocational skills
- personal development & creativity
- personal care

Vocational areas include horticulture, livestock husbandry, building and vehicle maintenance, catering and domestic services. Work experience is arranged for students as appropriate and students also have access to physical pursuits, the performing and creative arts and leisure facilities.

Towards independence and employment: Throughout the course, certain core skills are addressed to help students develop their self-confidence and self-awareness. Dilston offers each student opportunities for personal growth, development of general employability skills, acquisition of specific vocational skills, and increased independence and maturity.

Links with other establishments

NATSPEC, MENCAP Further Education Colleges, Newcastle FE College, work experience placements with local employers, local community education.

Out-of-term contact: During holiday times, MENCAP National Office 4, Swan Courtyard, Coventry Road, Birmingham B26 1BU. Tel: 0121 707 7877.

Doncaster College for the Deaf

Leger Way, Doncaster, South Yorkshire DN2 6AY
Tel: 01302 386700 voice/text Fax: 01302 361808
Website: www.yrsd-dcd.org.uk
E-mail: enquiries@yrsd-dcd.org.uk
Director: Mr H Heard   College Principal: Ms J Richardson
Catchment area: National   Age range: 16-59

COPE

Aims to provide comprehensive programmes of further and continuing education and training for deaf and hearing-impaired school-leavers and adults.

General description

The College is located on a residential campus near to Doncaster town centre, with easy access by road, rail or air. The college facilities are designed to reflect the real work environment across a wide range of industries and occupations, and our provision is tailored to meet the individual needs of over 200 students.

Accommodation is appropriate to the needs of each student, with on-campus halls of residence or houses and flats for the more mature students. It is a unique feature of Doncaster College for the Deaf that the vast majority of our 200-plus students are educated on campus. Experience has shown that most deaf students make greater progress and attain better results when working with other hearing impaired individuals, and receiving their tuition from specialist staff.

Communication: The college operates within Total Communication environment. Students receive tuition through a combination of speech and sign language to permit maximum acquisition of language and to allow students to gain confidence in their communication skills. To support our academic function we employ highly motivated and trained teams of residential social workers. The staff team has specialist skills for counselling deaf people. All students are nominated a key worker with whom they can develop a close relationship.

Applications for places: By application form (available from College Admissions Office), and interview with basic aptitude tests. Accepted students usually begin in the following September.

Students accepted: The college accepts students aged between 16 and 59 years, depending on age and the type of course proposed, sponsored either by their Local Education Authority (LEA), by the Further Education Funding Councils of England and Wales (FEFCs) or by the Training, Enterprise and Education Directorate (TEED). Training opportunities are open to all eligible people regardless of ethnic origin, sex or religion.

Courses and facilities

There are ten college departments providing courses in a diverse choice of subjects, offered either at academic levels or through vocational routes. A substantial range of courses are provided within these departments including: vocational access, applied technology, business studies and office technology, community studies (including catering and caring skills), construction (includes horticulture), creative arts (includes hairdressing), motor vehicle engineering and sport, recreation and leisure studies. Our language and communication department and mathematics department service the vocational courses.

Qualifications: All students have the opportunity to gain relevant nationally-recognised and validated qualifications such as BTEC, City & Guilds, Pitman, RSA, NVQs and GNVQs, GCSE and GCE AS and A levels.

Facilities: There are extensive, well-equipped teaching and training facilities, with specialist workshops designed both to meet the highest training standards and to recreate the real work environment. The College has superb sports and recreation facilities that include a modern sports hall, heated indoor swimming pool and extensive playing fields.

Dorincourt Centre

Oaklawn Road, Leatherhead, Surrey KT22 0BT
Tel: 01372 841300 Fax: 01372 843753
Website: www.dorincourt.org
Email: margaret.huxtable@dorincourt.org
Principal: Mrs Margaret Huxtable
Age range: 19-40
Catchment area: UK
Controlled by: Queen Elizabeth Foundation
Fees: Day care fee £35 per day; residential fees: £30,000 per year

Aims to provide a stimulating living skills centre with progressive arts and leisure facilities for severely disabled young people, giving the confidence and the skills to move on to a lifestyle of their choice.

General description

A purpose-built residential centre with single rooms and apartments suited to individual needs. The centre provides a comprehensive programme for each individual that will promote personal development, build confidence and achieve a realistic level of independence.

Courses and facilities

Dorincourt Centre provides each student with a two to three year programme which develops core skills essential for moving on to greater independence. A personal tutor and key worker system operates across the Centre.

An arts department gives students the opportunity to discover new skills and pursue creative interests in the visual and performing arts, plus information and communication technology.

A dedicated care team encourages individuals to manage their own care whilst providing a network of support.

Physiotherapy is available on site, responding to individual needs.

The Life Skills programme offers comprehensive training to individuals to support their move on from the centre.

The leisure department provides information and works with individuals to access sport and leisure opportunities both locally and nationally.

Dorton College of Further Education

COPE

Seal Drive, Seal, Sevenoaks, Kent TN15 0AH
Tel: 01732 592600 Fax: 01732 592601
Principal: Mike Morris
Managed by: Royal London Society for the Blind
Catchment area: National   Age range: 16+
Fees: College fees fall into a banded structure. Contact the College for current fee levels

Dorton College of Further Education is managed by the Royal London Society for the Blind and was established to provide a unique partnership between a specialist college and the further education sector. The objective was to create a syndicate that enables visually-impaired people to gain access to the widest range of provision on the basis of equality with their sighted peers. Partnerships with four sector colleges have now been established. This consortium is committed to equal opportunities and the principles outlined by the Kennedy committee in the report - Widening Participation. We also endorse the findings of the Tomlinson Committee - Inclusive Education - and work together to ensure that provision for visually-impaired people matches the individual needs of each student.

General description

Dorton College is a custom-built residential college for visually-impaired students based in a park-like setting, close to three main towns and only 35 minutes from London via British Rail. The College is fully resourced with specialist academic and learning support tutors, and equipment relevant to those with a visual impairment. Residential units consist of single study bedrooms with shared kitchen and bathroom facilities and students receive appropriate independent living skills training. Extended curriculum activities are an important part of college life and include a wide variety of sport and leisure pursuits and links with local interest groups, to develop personal and social competencies.

Students: Age 16+ and adults who are blind or partially-sighted. Students with additional disabilities will be accepted dependent on their assessed needs.

Application/selection: Informal visits are welcomed prior to any application for a place. Formal assessments are arranged and will usually take three days. Residential accommodation is available. Assessments are not competitive between students and if it is felt that a suitable course can be found, a place will be offered.

Courses and facilities

Dorton College provides a wide range of pre-vocational, vocational and academic studies through facilities on the Dorton Campus and via established partnership links with local colleges. Students attending local colleges for their chosen study have access to qualified and experienced specialist tutors, training and access to appropriate specialist equipment and full support in the classroom from Dorton College specialist staff. Dorton College prospectus provides further details about availability of courses and mainstream links.

49

Easter Anguston Residential Farm Training Centre

Peterculter, Aberdeen AB14 0PJ
Tel: 01224 733627
Principal Officer: Mrs Chris Stewart
Age range: Applications welcomed from 16 to 25-year-olds
Catchment area: All Scotland
Controlled by: Voluntary Service Aberdeen, 38 Castle Street, Aberdeen AB11 5YU
Fees: £282 per week residential fee. £132.46 per week training fee

Aims to provide a range of social and vocational training for young adults with learning difficulties in a working farm environment.

General description

Easter Anguston is a 70-acre working farm, located on the outskirts of Aberdeen and ten miles from the city centre, which provides opportunities for training in four main production units:

- horticulture
- livestock
- vegetables
- skills development.

Trainees live off-site in a core and cluster complex in the nearby village of Peterculter. Additionally, there are now two other properties in the village and one in Aberdeen itself, providing a range of semi-autonomous living areas.

Staffing: Five farm staff; nine residential care staff (five part-time and three full-time); one domestic assistant; a part-time social worker also provides a service to the trainees.

Students accepted: Easter Anguston is equipped to take up to 17 trainees with learning difficulties.

Applications/selection: Local authority social work department wishing to refer a client for admission to Easter Anguston must complete and forward to the Principal Officer up-to-date educational, medical, psychological and social background reports. Application forms are available from the Principal Officer.

Courses and facilities

Attendance at Easter Anguston Residential Farm Training Centre is not for a fixed duration. Through a system of annual progress reviews, the sponsoring local authority and Easter Anguston staff make a judgement as to whether the placement continues to be of benefit to the trainee.

The Enham Trust

Enham Alamein, Andover, Hampshire SP11 6JS
Tel: 01264 345800 Fax: 01264 351551
Catchment area: Nationwide   Age range: 16+
Controlled by: Independent charity
Fees: On application

Aims to provide the best opportunities available for people with disabilities to secure employment or worthwhile occupation with appropriate housing and support. The Enham Trust is a company and charity dedicated to assisting people with disabilities to lead progressive, fulfilled and independent lives. With over 80 years experience, Enham provides a comprehensive range of services designed to meet individual needs.

Courses and facilities

- Professional vocational assessment, work preparation and training programmes leading to National Vocational Qualifications.

- Business skills training in a purpose-built unit which provides marketing and related office services for internal and external customers.

- Full-time employment and training opportunities with Enham Industries in a variety of manufacturing environments.

- Supported Employment Programme providing jobs with employers over a wide geographical area.

- Programmes are available on a residential or daily basis.

- Occupational Day Programme providing an opportunity for individuals to progress towards independent living through a variety of work-based and other structured activities.

- Residential care facilities for people with physical disabilities.

Vocational Programme: Lindsey Brewer, Senior Development Officer

Occupational Programmes: Deirdre Lias, Manager – Occupational Programmes

Residential Care: Marie Allen, General Manager – Housing and Care Services

Exhall Grange School

Wheelwright Lane, Ash Green, Coventry, Warwickshire CV7 9HP
Tel: 02476 364200 Fax: 02476 645055
Headteacher: R G Bignell BA, MUniv
Catchment area: No restrictions   Age range: 16-19
Controlled by: Warwickshire County Council
Fees: Available on request

COPE

Aims to produce confident, caring and resourceful young people by recognising their equal worth and developing their full potential.

General description

The school is situated on a spacious, well-planned, attractive 35-acre site on the northern edge of Coventry. The school consists of extensive modern buildings including suites of classrooms for English, mathematics, modern languages and the humanities. There is an extensive Resources Centre including libraries, four laboratories, three technology workrooms and a 'state-of-the-art' food technology suite. ICT is regarded as a priority, and the school is bidding for Specialist Technology College Status. There is a swimming pool and sports field, and its fine reputation in sport led to the award of the Sportsmark Gold Award in 1999.

Staffing: Staff/student ratio is 1:5. Teaching staff are all experienced teachers, who have, or are currently working for, their additional qualification to teach visually impaired students. There are also special educational assistants and a range of support staff.

Students accepted: Pupils from the age of 2 years. Blind, partially sighted and/or physically impaired of all abilities. The sixth form has up to 40 male and female students. Priority Special Educational Needs provided for are visual impairment, physical disability and medical needs. All students benefit from individualised timetabling, specialist teaching and the latest technology.

Applications/selections: Applicants must come via sponsoring LEA. Informal visits welcome. Selection based on assessment and available reports. There is an annual Open Day and regular visitors mornings. Informal visits are welcome with every effort being made to facilitate short stay assessments prior to entry.

Courses and facilities

Exhall Grange has a well-equipped health centre, physiotherapy and hydrotherapy department on site. Supporting professionals include GPs, speech therapists, educational and clinical psychologists, ophthalmologists, optometrists and dietitians.

Students between 16 and 19 can choose to join the open sixth form and take courses leading to further or specialist further education, university entrance, training or employment.

GNVQ can be followed at:

a) Foundation level for those students who need the opportunity to further build their self-confidence and basic skills through individual programmes in order to prepare for adult life or further specialist education

b) Intermediate level for those students who have some achievement at GCSE level and wish to prepare for vocational courses, training schemes or employment

c) Advanced level for those students who have already completed their Intermediate level or those who wish to study in a vocational way at a higher level.

For those who are not yet ready for a GNVQ course we offer the City & Guilds Skillpower course.

Academic courses leading to A or AS level are available in a range of subjects including chemistry, biology, physics, history, geography, English literature, mathematics, music, French and art. Some students follow a mixture of vocational courses and work closely with local colleges which provide courses that are less in demand.

Links with other establishments

Exhall Grange works in partnership with North Warwickshire & Hinckley College and King Edward VI Form College which enables a wider range of A levels and vocational courses to be offered. It also has close links with Mid Warwickshire and South Warwickshire Colleges, and local industry-based companies which are used for work experience and visits relating to many of its courses. Agencies including RNIB, SENSE and VIEW have buildings on the school site.

Fairfield Opportunity Farm

Dilton Marsh, Westbury, Wiltshire BA13 4DL
Tel: 01373 823028
Managing Director: Mr B A K Hester MBE
Principal: Janet Kenwood
Age range: 16-25
Catchment area: Wiltshire, national and international
Controlled by: Independent charity
Fees: Reviewed annually in September; are currently £20,634 (1999/2000). Normally met by contributions from the FEFC, local authority and DSS benefits.

Aims to provide education, training and care for young adults with learning disabilities with the objectives of preparing them for employment and a more independent lifestyle. These courses can be day or residential.

General description

The college is situated on a 25-acre farm in the rural village of Dilton Marsh, some two miles from Westbury and six miles from Trowbridge. As well as the usual farm buildings, there is a craft/woodwork department, two classrooms each equipped with a computer, an engineering workshop, a horticulture department, stabling and an outdoor riding arena, as well as a large recreation hall for social and leisure activities. Five houses situated within the village provide comfortable homes for students.

Staffing: College - Principal, residential care manager, senior tutor, 8 qualified teachers/tutors, 2 residential care supervisors, 8 full-time support workers. Administration - company secretary and administrative assistant.

Students accepted: Young adults usually aged from 16 to 25 whose disabilities can range from moderate to severe. Older applicants may be considered subject to availability of places. All potential students must attend a one-week assessment period before a place can be offered.

Applications/selection: Parents may either contact Janet Kenwood direct, or make arrangements for a careers officer or social worker to apply on their behalf; a visit to the college can then be arranged. A brochure is available on request.

Courses and facilities

Training is arranged on an individual basis and the course duration is normally two years. A personal tutor/keyworker system is operated, which involves each individual student in the compilation of their own Individual Learning Plan whilst still satisfying the FEFC educational criteria. Fairfield is an approved centre for NVQs, NPTC, Asdan and Wordpower/Numberpower, covering a range of subjects within Independent Living as well as vocational option subjects in horticulture, craftwork, equestrian studies, farming or engineering. Makaton signing is used when required. Swimming, gym and other recreational and social activities are also arranged for students whilst at Fairfield.

Links with other establishments

Students in their second year access complementary courses at Trowbridge College.

Farleigh College

Farleigh Hungerford, Nr Bath, Somerset BA3 6RW
Tel: 01225 753130 Fax: 01225 756921
Website: www.nhh4as.co.uk
Email: brads@zetnet.co.uk
Principal: Mr Stephen Bradshaw
Age Range: 10-18
Catchment area: UK
Controlled by: Farleigh Schools Ltd
Fees: Available on request

Farleigh College caters for students with Asperger's Syndrome whose needs cannot be catered for within their own Local Education Authority.

Courses and facilities

Curriculum: All have access to the full National Curriculum. External accreditation through GCSE and COA.

Eclectic approach: Farleigh College recognises the value of an eclectic approach utilising the valuable programmes such as multi-sensory, TEACCH approach, Instrumental Enrichment, Somerset Thinking Skills and the Social Use of Language Programme. Extensively supported by IT.

Specialist input: The college has an excellent well qualified support team involving an educational psychologist, a speech and language therapist and an occupational therapist, GP and a counsellor.

Residential: The college has a full care staff team who look after the pupils in five separate living areas as well as supporting the students whilst in the classroom. There are study bedrooms as well as larger rooms. All living areas are based upon a family unit to provide a safe, secure, warm, friendly environment where the students can develop understanding and empathy towards their peers.

Staffing: There is a teaching staff ratio of 3:1 with maximum class sizes of eight. The full staff team at Farleigh College is 70 giving a 1:1 ratio. There is a staff-training programme to ensure all staff have a thorough understanding and awareness of Asperger's Syndrome so that they can confidently and comprehensively meet the needs of our pupils.

Students accepted: Students with Asperger's Syndrome.

Application: Referral direct to the college.

Links with other establishments

24-hour Curriculum: Extensive use is made of the local area including the sports facilities at Bath, Trowbridge and Bradford on Avon as well as the climbing and walking on the Mendip Hills. The extensive grounds of the school with access to lake and 200 acres of parkland allow the school to develop individual leisure plans for each pupil.

Finchale Training College

Durham, DH 1 5RX
Tel: 0191 386 2634 Fax: 0191 386 4962
Principal: Dr D Etheridge
Catchment area: UK   Age range: 18-62
Controlled by: Independent charity

Aims to provide vocational rehabilitation and training for people with disabilities and special needs and help them regain confidence through employment.

General description

A residential training centre with residential, classroom and workshop accommodation of a high standard, so that disabled people are able to care for themselves with maximum independence. There are nursing, welfare and counselling facilities, and trainees are encouraged to organise their own leisure activities.

Staffing: Training staff are experienced personnel from commerce and industry who are dedicated to passing on their skills to their students. The staff to student ratio in training is 1:15, some classes are even smaller.

Students accepted: All disabilities except severe sensory disabilities.

Applications/selection: Apply through the Local Disability Employment Adviser. Application should be accompanied by full medical reports. Students are sponsored by the DfEE and usually attend under Work-based Learning for Adults or Work Preparation, but other sponsors can be accommodated.

Courses and facilities

Finchale provides a high standard of vocational rehabilitation and training in a wide range of skills.

- Horticulture (amenity and commercial) - up to twelve month course, practical and theoretical to NVQ levels 1-3.

- Estimating - up to one-year course to convert a building tradesman/woman who cannot continue with site work, to this profession which is in great demand. NVQ level 3.

- Wood occupations - up to six months' training in practical woodworking skills to NVQ levels 1-3.

- Servicing Electrical Appliances - up to 40 weeks studying repair of washing machines, microwaves, fridges, freezers, etc. NVQ level 2.

- Computer Servicing - 46 weeks learning to repair printers, disk drives and computers to NVQ levels 2-3 with an additional option in Networking and Internet Operations.

- Electronics Servicing - up to one year of modern electronics from security alarms to robots and logic circuits to NVQ level 2.

- Accounting - up to one year's training to Association of Accounting Technicians levels 2 and 3.

- Administration - training up to one year in office skills at NVQ levels 1-3.

- Distribution and Warehousing Operations with forklift truck training - up to 38 weeks training to NVQ level 2.

- Purchasing - up to 52 weeks training to NVQ level 2.

Out-of-term contact: Training is continuous except at Bank Holidays, for approximately ten days over Christmas and New Year, and for two weeks closure in the Spring and Summer.

Fortune Centre of Riding Therapy

Avon Tyrrell, Bransgore, Nr Christchurch, Dorset, BH23 8EE
Tel: 01425 673297 Fax: 01425 674320
Director: Mrs J Dixon-Clegg
Catchment area: Unrestricted   Age range: 16-25
Controlled by: Voluntary - Registered Charity No. 1045352 Co. Ltd by Guarantee No. 3031713
Fees: Supported by either FEFC or Social Services department

Offers education, occupation training and rehabilitation, using horses as medium.

General description

Two separate establishments in the New Forest - one residential for all students and the other where they work daily. Indoor and outdoor riding schools at each location. Tutorial rooms, fields for sports. Access to evening classes locally and recreational facilities.

Staffing: 17 teachers (riding therapist and educational); nine full-time care staff; one occupational therapist; three nurses, one part-time physiotherapist and seven administration and finance staff; plus additional supporting staff.

Students accepted: Up to 30 lesser disabled young people, male and female, with learning difficulties, emotional disturbance and/or mild physical disability.

Applications/selection: Admission procedure: initial visit, one-day assessment, residential seven-day assessment - usually takes place during the summer and autumn terms for entry in the following autumn term.

Courses and facilities

Residential further education through horsemastership (two years), which teaches life and social skills to young people with special needs, using a horse-based extended curriculum. These courses are designed to extend basic education, social and lifeskills, to improve confidence, maturity and self-esteem, whilst offering a therapeutic environment and engendering occupational skills. The course offers NVQ 1 and 2 in Horsecare, BHS progressive tests and stage exams, City and Guilds Wordpower and Numberpower, ASDAN Workright and ASDAN Towards Independence.

Links with other establishments

Access to local evening classes and recreation centre.

Out-of-term contact: The Administrator - the Centre never closes.

Fourways Assessment Unit

Cleworth Hall Lane, Tyldesley, Manchester M29 8NT
Tel: 01942 870841 Fax: 01942 875958
Manager: Christine Pilling
Catchment area: Unrestricted   Age range: 18 +
Controlled by: Wigan Metropolitan Borough Social Services Department
Fees: Current fees available from Manager

Aims to assess potential for independent living, employment, training, etc and to provide activities and experience aimed at helping young people to mature and develop satisfying life styles.

General description

Accommodation for residential service users is in single rooms containing purpose-built furniture; lifts; flat(s) for practice/teaching in independent living. Many people go home for weekends. Sports facilities, horseriding, basketball, swimming, Duke of Edinburgh award courses. Various social occasions at Leigh College.

Staffing: Manager, programme organiser; three assistant accommodation managers, three senior instructors; three full-time and four part-time day care assistants; three full-time and one part-time night care assistants; four support workers; domestics; kitchen staff; drivers; nurse; physiotherapy/occupational/speech therapy sessions; consultant.

Students accepted: Physical disabilities/head injuries - severity no bar, providing there is no need for nursing care beyond that which would be provided in their own homes or by a domiciliary nursing service. Cannot accept maladjusted or severely emotionally disturbed applicants. Ability range moderate learning difficulties and upwards. Mixed sex. Head-injured young people are accepted and moderate behaviour problems accommodated.

Applications/selection: Forms from Manager. Informal visits by arrangement.

Courses and facilities

Service users stay for a maximum of two years. Specific teaching in social/life skills/computer aided learning.

At local colleges (Wigan and Leigh): A wide variety of courses from special needs to mainstream. Programmes tailored to individuals.

At Fourways: Specialist individual tuition. Individualised rehabilitation programmes.

Fourways Computer Publishing Centre: A unit attached to Fourways providing short courses (residential or day) covering wordprocessing, spreadsheets, desktop publishing and systems management. Specialist lecturers are at the Unit, along with six disabled unit leaders to assist with problems that any student may encounter.

Links with other establishments

With Leigh and Wigan College as instanced above.

Out-of-term contact: Christine Pilling (Manager) available all year.

Furze Mount

Copthorne Road, Upper Colwyn Bay, Clwyd LL28 5YP.
Tel: 01492 532679 Fax: 01492 531280
Officer-in-Charge: Ms Sharon Edwards
Age range: 18 +
Catchment area: Nationwide
Controlled by: Mental Health Care UK Ltd.

Aims to maximise self competence through exposure to appropriate experiences.

General description

Located in residential area of Colwyn Bay, North Wales. Previously a private residence, it stands in its own mature grounds.

Staffing: A high ratio of staff to clients. Care, education and nursing staff, consultant psychiatrist; medical officer; educational psychologist and speech therapist.

Students accepted: Adults with severe learning difficulties, with peripheral disabilities considered individually. Non-ambulant can be accepted. Male and female registered 24.

Applications/selection: Initial contact via telephone or letter to Heather Brown, Alexander House, Highfield Park, Llandyrnog, Denbigh, Denbighshire LL16 4LU Tel: 01824 790 600; Fax: 01824 700 341. Interviews and visits can also be arranged through the home manager.

Courses and facilities

Furze Mount is based on the view that people with severe learning difficulties derive greater stimulation and a higher rate of overall personal development when exposed to an environment which stretches individual potential. It is possible to cater for life care, though consideration will also be given to clients requiring specific long or short term programmes, together with rotating care.

To plan individual treatment, an assessment of each individual's need and potential is carried out by a multi-disciplinary team consisting of senior education, nursing and care staff, together with the consultant psychiatrist, medical officer and educational psychologist, where appropriate.

All residents are exposed to appropriate experiences both within and external to the establishment in pursuit of increased self-competence. Emphasis is placed on creating stability within social groups.

Links with other establishments

Interchange has commenced with Llandrillo College of Further Education.

Garvald
West Linton

Dolphinton, Nr West Linton, Borders, Scotland EH46 7HJ
Tel: 01968 682211 Fax: 01968 682611
Principal: Mr Martin Dawson
Catchment area: Nationwide   Age range: 16 +
Controlled by: An independent centre. Registered with Scottish
Borders Social Work Department
Fees: £369 per week

Aims to provide residential care, training and further education based on the principles of Rudolf Steiner.

General description

An independent centre run on the principles of Rudolf Steiner. Situated 20 miles south of Edinburgh in a rural setting, but within easy reach of local towns. Seven different workshop/training areas and a developed further education programme. Accommodation in four hostels, one in the main house and three separate houses in the grounds. Mainly single rooms with some double. Students are encouraged to further develop social skills by visiting neighbouring towns.

Staffing: 37 staff. Including 21care staff; workshop leaders, gardeners, handymen; office staff; teachers; speech therapist.

Students accepted: Those with a wide range of learning difficulties. 32 students. All ambulant.

Applications/selection: By letter to Principal in first instance.

Courses and facilities

Training activities: woodwork, bakery, weavery, crafts, laundry, kitchen work, estate management.

Garvald is in partnership with Borders College. Accreditation in the different training activities can be achieved via participation in our modular training programme.

Further education subjects: current affairs, topic lesson, physical education, music, painting.

The 60-acre estate provides many training and leisure opportunities.

Links with other establishments

Member of: Committee for Steiner Special Education, Scottish Association for Curative Education and Social Therapy.

Garvald Centre Edinburgh

2 Montpelier Terrace, Edinburgh EH10 4NF
Tel: 0131 228 3712 Fax: 0131 229 1468
Catchment area: No restrictions   Age range: 17 +
Controlled by: Garvald Training Centre Ltd
Fees: Contact Administrator (Day Centre/Residential)

Inspired by the ideas of Rudolph Steiner, Garvald Centre provides day and residential services to people who have a learning disability. In striving to build a community together, we recognise and value the uniqueness of each person and seek to create a quality of environment, activities and social relationships which foster the realisation of individual potential.

General description

We offer a therapeutic environment in which individuals with a range of learning disabilities can take steps in their development towards maturity, and can be supported in finding their place in relation to the wider community. We have three community houses, two workshop buildings and a shop. The greater part of each day is spent doing creative work and producing quality articles; as part of our work we do our own catering and healthy nutrition is encouraged. Additionally there are opportunities for continuing education, therapy and further education at local colleges. Festivals are celebrated throughout the year with plays and other activities.

Staffing: Garvald has a staff of 60+.

Numbers accepted: We have places for 28 residents and 100 trainees. Mixed sexes.

Applications/selection: Contact the Administrator for an application form, also to be completed by your Local Authority's social worker.

Courses and facilities

Our day activities include: bakery & confectionery; joinery; pottery; printing/stained glass; puppet-making/puppetry; metal work and Tools of Self Reliance; weaving; education; speech therapy; eurhythmy. Our eight buildings are situated in the south west area of Edinburgh.

Links with other establishments

Links with other organisations whose work is based on the ideas of Rudolf Steiner, including other Garvald ventures around Edinburgh and the Borders.

Out-of-term contact: Office open.

George House

Swalcliffe Park School, Swalcliffe, Nr. Banbury, Oxon OX15 5EP
Tel: 01295 780302 Fax: 01295 780006
Principal: Ray Hooper
Catchment area: Nationwide   Age range: 16 +
Controlled by: Board of Trustees. Board of Governors.
Fees: £38,670 per annum

Aims to encourage a high level of independence, personal growth and the acquisition of life and vocational skills.

General description

A purpose-built unit situated in the grounds of Swalcliffe Park. Completely independent from the main school, has its own high standard of accommodation and equipment, and a high staffing ratio. It is designed to allow either group living or, for those who are capable, of living independently. Six of the rooms are single bedsit type, fully furnished with toilet and shower en suite and one of these is designed to accommodate a disabled person.

The remaining rooms are shared by two boys. Meals are prepared either by staff or boys in one or more of the three fully equipped kitchens. Laundry is done in token-operated commercial machines situated within the building. A student common room, bathroom and two staff flats complete the complex.

Staffing: Care leader; deputy; assistant; teaching-unit teacher; access to, and use made of, specialist teachers from main school.

Students accepted: Boys who are socially and educationally disadvantaged.

Applications/selection: Individual interviews.

Courses and facilities

An emphasis on lifeskills and independent living. Linked to school practice in general subjects. Local technical college courses. Work experience.

Links with other establishments

North Oxon College and other local colleges.

61

The Grange Centre for People with Disabilities

Rectory Lane, Bookham, Surrey KT23 4DZ
Tel: 01372 452608 Fax: 01372 451959
Director: Paul H Wood
Catchment area: Nationwide   Age range: 18 +
Controlled by: Council of Management
Fees: On application - dependent upon type of placement

General description

Accommodation in either semi-independent flats and bedsitters, shared flats or single rooms in main house, according to need and ability. Annexe for elderly and physically infirm.

Staffing: Director; deputy director; secretary; 10 care staff (non-medical); 4 workshop staff (teaching embroidery, dressmaking and horticulture); handyman; housekeeping; cooking and cleaning staff; social skills teacher and clerical support staff.

Students accepted: Either sex. Some physically disabled, some with learning disabilities.

Application/selection: Forms from the Grange Centre. Informal visits by prospective resident and parents or social worker welcomed. One day assessment. Two-week residential assessment including residential middle weekend. Currently a waiting list.

Courses and facilities

The Grange Centre offers workskills training in embroidery, dressmaking and horticulture, also a craft centre teaching a wide range of crafts. Skills training also available in office skills, retailing skills, catering skills and computer skills. A wide range of life and social skills are taught.

Links with other establishments

Anticipated City & Guilds for needlecraft and horticulture and in life skills and social skills.

Out-of-term contact: We do not close for holidays.

Grange Village Community

Littledean Road, Newnham, Gloucestershire GL14 1HJ
Tel: 01594 516246 Fax: 01594 516969
Website: www.camphill.org.uk
Catchment area: Unrestricted   Age range: 21-25
Controlled by: Camphill Village Trust; a recognised sheltered workshop

COPE

A working community with adults, some of whom have special needs - real, meaningful work; a shared family life; a rich cultural context.

General description

Between 5 and 7 residents live in family houses with co-workers and their children. Festivals are celebrated and there is a very wide range of evening activities: study groups, lectures, dancing, games, music acting, reading etc.

Students accepted: 40 men and women with learning disabilities.

Application/selection: Applications to The Admissions Group, Grange Village, Newnham, Glos GL14 1HJ can be made at the age of 18 onwards. Being put on the waiting list is not joining a queue. The particular needs of each applicant awaiting admission are considered. The waiting list is only made up of those who have had a successful trial visit. Visits are arranged as soon as possible after interview, usually for a fortnight initially, then for a three-month period when accommodation is available.

Courses and facilities

No courses as such are provided, the Village being a community within which each resident can be assisted to individual independence and social adjustment.

Links with other establishments

Close ties with the local village and other Camphill Communities.

Out-of-term contact: Not necessary. Information is always available from the Village. The Village does not close at any time of the year.

Grenville College

Bideford, North Devon EX39 3JR
Tel: 01237 472212 Fax: 01237 477020
Email: info@grenville.devon.sch.uk
Website: www.grenvile.devon.sch.uk
Principal: M C V Cane BSc, PhD, MRSC
Catchment area: Nationwide   Age range: 2½-18
Controlled by: Woodard Corporation
Fees per term: £4110 max (full boarding and tuition); £3082
max (weekly boarding and tuition); £385 (special English tuition)

To help all pupils, including those with specific learning difficulties/
dyslexia, to achieve their potential academically and in other ways, via
extra-curricular activities, to provide a broad education founded upon a
sound moral basis.

General description

Co-educational boarding and day school for pupils aged 2½ - 18. The school provides extensive playing fields and excellent sports facilities together with a wide variety of activities including music, drama and art. Special emphasis is placed on club activities and the school is one of only four in the South West to have its own Operating Authority Licence to issue awards for the Duke of Edinburgh's Award Scheme.

Students accepted: A full secondary curriculum is provided for boys aged 11 to 18. Entrants, including those with specific learning difficulties/dyslexia, may join at sixth form level.

The dyslexic 6th form student: The student will have an adviser from Grenville's long established dyslexia unit who will be able to offer support and advice. If necessary, lessons can be timetabled with the adviser for specific work in areas such as study skills, reading techniques and spelling. Re-take English GCSE is available. The student is also welcome to make use of the dyslexia unit during private study periods and to benefit from the computer facilities. A level and GNVQ teaching is carried out in small groups by staff with long experience and expertise in teaching dyslexic students. In 1999, A level dyslexic candidates

achieved a pass rate of 100% pass rate at both A level and GNVQ, many with distinctions and merits. Finally, the pastoral system is carefully designed to be of help to the dyslexic student. Tutor groups are small, about eight students, and they meet regularly.

Applications/selection: Parents of dyslexic applicants are asked to submit an educational psychologist's report prior to a child's interview and testing at Grenville. All entrants are expected to be of at least average intelligence and capable of following academic courses to GCSE level. Relevant GCSE passes at grade C are necessary for entry to A level courses. Enquiries to the Registrar.

Courses and facilities

A course brochure is available on request.

GCSE and Advanced level courses. Intermediate and Advanced level GNVQ courses in Business are also provided.

Grenville College has a recently-built science and library block, a language laboratory, well-equipped design and technology workshops, art rooms and a music school. A modern assembly hall/chapel not only provides a centre for worship but also has excellent facilities for dramatic and musical productions.

All sixth formers receive guidance and advice on their choice of higher education courses and careers as part of the weekly timetable. In addition they have access to a wide selection of reference books in the careers library and ECCTIS 2000.

Links with other establishments

Grenville maintains informal links with FE colleges and universities. A considerable number of dyslexic pupils go on to higher education.

The Hatch (Camphill Community)

St Johns House, Kington Lane, Thornbury, Bristol BS35 1NA.
Tel: 01454 413010 Fax: 01454 414705
Website: www.camphill.org.uk
Catchment area: Unrestricted   Age range: 18-30
Controlled by: A group of managers
Fees: £447 per week as of April '99

Aims for the integration of each young person into a worthwhile working situation, the cultivation of mutual social awareness and encouragement to participate in various cultural activities.

General description

The Hatch Community comprises four residential houses, providing a therapeutic living situation where staff members, their families and residents live together. A bio-dynamically run farm and garden provide essential working activity alongside a weaving and woodwork shop, as well as domestic tasks. Recreational, sporting and cultural activities include the use of facilities in Thornbury, a market town. Christian festivals are an integral part of the life.

Staffing: Eight permanent co-workers with years of experience of living and working in Camphill Communities and at least eight other helpers, receiving in-service training.

Students accepted: Young adults with learning disabilities, male and female.

Applications/selection: On receipt of our questionnaire including past relevant medical and school reports, an interview with experienced staff members is arranged. A two-four week trial period is offered when space is available. Long stay places arise as older residents move on to more permanent places.

Courses and facilities

The Hatch provides basic work training as opposed to formal further education. The emphasis is upon individual guidance in work as therapy. In addition to daily living skills, guided work experience is offered in landwork, cooking, laundry and other domestic tasks.

   The overall duration of placement is individually considered with regard to the young person's needs and their ongoing development and maturation.

   There are eight fixed holiday weeks in the year. Families, friends etc are welcome to visit by arrangement.

Links with other establishments

All other Camphill Communities and other local similar establishments.

Out-of-term contact: The Secretary, The Sheiling School, Thornbury (01454) 412194.

65

The Helen Allison School

Longfield Road, Meopham, Kent DA13 0EW
Tel: 01474 814878 Fax: 01474 812033
E mail: helen.allison@nas.org.uk
Principal: Jacqui Ashton-Smith
Age range: 16-19
Catchment area: No restrictions except travelling distance.
Controlled by: The National Autistic Society.
Fees: Day students £25,218.96 per annum + VAT
Weekly boarders £37,518.99 per annum + VAT

To provide education modified to meet the specific needs of children and young adults with autism and Asperger's Syndrome in a safe and structured environment to enable them to reach their fullest potential and to prepare them for adulthood.

Courses and facilities

The Jubilee Unit provides continuing education with a programme appropriate for pupils with autism and Asperger's Syndrome.

Students accepted: Diagnosed as being on the autistic continuum.

Applications/selection: Applications via local education authority. Selection panel - Principal and consultant psychiatrist.

Henshaw's College

Bogs Lane, Harrogate, North Yorkshire HG1 4ED
Tel: 01423 886451 Fax: 01423 885095
Principal: J Cole
Catchment area: Nationwide   Age range: 16 +
Controlled by: Henshaw's Society for the Blind

COPE

Our main aim is to enable students to identify and work towards achieving their long-term personal, social and vocational objectives.

General description

The College is situated on the outskirts of Harrogate on its own 12 acre campus. It is within easy walking distance of Starbeck Village, which has a variety of shops. A range of accommodation is available on campus to give students the opportunity to experience a variety of living options. All students benefit from the excellent facilities available in our Sport and Leisure complex. A wide choice of recreational activities is available during evenings and weekends both on and off campus. Students may participate in Special Olympics events at regional, national and international levels.

Students accepted: Students are visually impaired, many having additional physical or learning difficulties, or hearing impairment. Students come from all areas of the UK.

Applications/selection: We encourage prospective students, their parents and professionals to visit the College before making an application.

Courses and facilities

Our course-centred approach ensures that each student has the correct balance of subjects within a structured programme and access to a range of teaching approaches to support learning. Every student is assured of an appropriate peer group in both the teaching and learning environments and social settings. Provision is structured to meet the range and complexity of students' needs. Each student has his or her own individual timetable, with regular reviews ensuring that changing needs are met. Our curriculum extends into out-of-college hours and so encompasses all aspects of daily life. This holistic approach helps reinforce the transference of skills learnt in the classroom into everyday living.

The core curriculum provides the skills for adult life and independent living, together with pre-vocational and vocational education, training and guidance. Courses are accredited through a range of external awarding bodies. All students receive careers advice to explore realistic future options. Work experience provides opportunities to gain confidence and apply skills, whilst craft workshops help develop key skills for work. Vocational courses are available on campus and in conjunction with local mainstream colleges.

Care and Support

Physiotherapy, speech therapy and occupational therapy are available on campus, with counselling and psychological services arranged where needed.

Students are encouraged to make their own decisions and choices with support from their Key Worker and Personal Tutor to help them identify and achieve personal goals.

Long Term Solutions to Long Term Needs

Henshaw's Arts and Crafts Centre, together with our Community Housing, provide options for students leaving College but wishing to remain in the Harrogate area. This provision enables them to continue both their independence and vocational training as clients of Henshaw's in environments which provide appropriate staffing and resources.

Out-of-term contact: Vice Principal or Marketing & Liaison officer.

Hereward College

> Bramston Crescent, Tile Hall Lane, Coventry CV4 9SW
> Tel: 024 7646 1231 Fax: 024 7669 430
> Website: www.hereward.ac.uk
> Email: enquiries@hereward.ac.uk
> Principal: Mrs C Cole BA
> Age range: 16+
> Catchment area: Nationwide; overseas students also accepted
> Status: Incorporated FE Sector College (FEFC)
> Fees: On application, according to individual assessment.
> Majority of students FEFC funded

Aims to provide inclusive and integrated further education that allows disabled students to study alongside their non-disabled peers.

General description

Situated in Coventry, Hereward is in an urban environment with many local amenities. The college has close links with its local community and neighbouring FE colleges, enabling residential students to access additional learning and leisure experiences with support as required. Local non-residential students are welcome.

Staff qualifications and selection: The college employs some 160 staff with expertise in teaching and learning, care and enabling, nursing, therapies, counselling, education psychology and enabling technology. Hereward is an Investor in People and is accredited to the BSI/ISO 9002 quality standard.

Students accepted: The college supports students with a wide range of physical and/or sensory disabilities, delicate or complex medical conditions, specific or moderate learning difficulties, communication difficulties, brain and spinal injuries and autistic spectrum disorders. Local disabled and non-disabled students welcome.

Applications/selection: Regular visits and open events are offered. Disabled applicants invited to comprehensive assessment including overnight stay for prospective residential students. Decisions regarding admission are taken by a multi-disciplinary team based on an assessment of the benefit of a placement to the prospective student and the impact of admission on the experience of other learners.

Courses and facilities

The curriculum encompasses business studies, creative studies (including the performing arts), media studies, applied science (including information technology and sports), and residential education. Academic and vocational options from entry level to level 3 are available, including GCSEs, A levels, GNVQs, NVQs and Access courses. A degree programme in Fine Art/textiles is offered in conjunction with the University of Leeds at Bretton Hall. Basic skills support is available in all areas.

Learning resources include a vocational business studies centre, fully equipped TV and photographic studios, a learning resources centre, a large creative studies department including a multimedia suite, science and IT labs. Enabling technology is used extensively throughout.

24 hour medical, care and educational enabling services are available. Physiotherapy, speech therapy and conductive education are provided according to need. The student services centre houses careers, employment and HE guidance services, personal counselling and advice on welfare and benefits. Hereward's ACCESS centre where students' needs are assessed and appropriate technical and study support needs identified.

Links with other establishments

Hereward seeks to enhance opportunities for students through collaborative links with employers and other establishments. This currently involves work with the National Institute of Conductive Education, Jaguar Cars Ltd, the University of Leeds at Bretton Hall, Coventry's Youth Service, and three local FE colleges. The college works closely with Coventry's Quality Careers Service Ltd, giving students access to specialist careers advice and a wide range of work experience placements.

Out-of-term contact: Mike Thompson, Head, Student Services and Marketing.

Hesley Village College

Hesley Stripe Road, Tickhill, Doncaster, South Yorkshire DN11 9HH
Tel: 01302 868313 Fax: 01302 864059
Head: Mr S Ekins, Med, Dip(SpEd)
Catchment area: Nationwide   Age range: 16+
Controlled by: The Hesley Group, The Coach House, Hesley
Hall, Tickhill, Doncaster, South Yorkshire DN11 9HH.
Tel: 01302 866906 Fax: 01302 865473
Fees: On request from the Head

The Hesley Village College is a residential college for students with challenging behaviours as a result of autism and/or severe learning difficulties.

Newly opened in 1999, the college at present offers 22 fully residential placements for young people of 16+. A village development situated next to the college is planned for future years.

The aim of all Hesley Group schools and colleges is to enable people with special needs to achieve their full potential. The college's philosophy is based on the principles of Gentle Teach, an approach to managing challenging behaviour based on non-aversive positive intervention, as advocated by The Institute of Applied Behaviour Analysis (USA).

We seek to understand the behaviour, to identify its function and, by teaching alternative, more appropriate ways of achieving that function, aim to reduce the severity and frequency of the challenging behaviour.

General description

Hesley Village College is a Registered Home (1984 Act) and will be seeking FEFC accreditation during the year 2000. It is set in a magnificent Victorian mansion house within 100 acres of park and farmland. During the next several years, the Village proper will take shape within the grounds when a number of amenities such as shops, café and a village hall will be developed.

Courses and facilities

We want all our students to achieve their full potential and to live as independently as possible. We can help them by working on changing behaviours and developing age-appropriate related skills. All our courses are specially designed to help develop personal life skills which can lead to an attainable life plan. We are developing modular courses usually lasting for three years (which can be extended to meet individual needs) to cover continuous learning, dignified living, social integration and behavioural therapy.

Students accepted: 22 residential placements. Future numbers will be governed by the building of the Village housing.

Referrals and admissions: A student cannot be considered for a placement until an official request is received from the LEA, Social Services, or other referring agency. However, parents are encouraged to visit on an informal basis so that they can meet staff and students.

Parent partnership: The school is a strong advocate of teamwork between all agencies, and especially the student's parents and family. Contact is maintained through regular phone calls, visits home and visits by parents to the school.

Links with the community: This is an essential part of the daily life of our students, and includes leisure pursuits – skating, horse-riding, swimming, and bowling – and social training, when they will visit local shops and learn to use public transport and other amenities. Many of our students will also access courses at the local FE colleges.

Work experience: A major focus of the college is to provide our students with a variety of learning experiences which are relevant to work-based activities. Students will undertake a variety of work-based mini-enterprise activities as preparation for attending work experience projects with approved employers or schemes.

Hinwick Hall College of Further Education

Hinwick, Nr Wellingborough, Northants NN29 7JD
Tel: 01933 312470 Fax: 01933 412476
Principal: Mr E E Sinott MSc
Catchment area: No restrictions   Age range: 16-19 +
Controlled by: The Shaftesbury Society
Fees: Funding determined following assessement, and in agreement with the FEFC funding methodology. Support needs range from: £25,350 - £50,950

Preparation for an effective adulthood - vocational, occupational, advocacy skills, independence and social skills at individual, pairs and group levels. Opportunities to live and learn in one of nine fully equipped flats.

General description

Founded in 1943, the college is part of the national provision of the Shaftesbury Society. It is situated in a beautiful part of North Bedfordshire. The Hall itself is a Grade II listed building, and the College is an FEFC Grade I inspection. There are extensive grounds and provision for young people with disabilities. The main cross-college courses are the lifestyle courses and there are nine purpose built flats to reinforce independence and social skills.

Staffing: Lecturing - 12 staff; full nursing and care staff with three night staff. Learning support determined at assessment.

Students accepted: 40+ students. Mixed sex. All disabilities other than blind.

Applications/selection: Informal visit and tour. Two-day residential/assessment. Normal entry time beginning of September but other times acceptable in certain circumstances.

Courses and facilities

The courses have been planned to allow students to progress at the pace and level suitable to their abilities, and to enable them to fulfil their potential at a level which will bring success and self esteem in an adult environment. Courses are normally for three years, and are delivered through the following curriculum areas.

Core Skills which underpin the learning of all students: language, numeracy, money management and computer awarenesss.

Life Skills which reinforce the Core Skills, and develop everyday skills for the students' chosen lifestyles: social skills, flat management, meal preparation, money handling and leisure.

Creative Arts through which certain elements of Life Skills and Key Skills may be reinforced and tracked: textiles, multi-craft, music, drama and horticultre.

World of Work: a course designed internally to investigate the theory and practice of the workplace. Accreditation is through the ASDAN Workright Scheme.

Opportunities for learning throughout the full residential placement are supported by: physiotherapy, speech and language therapy, self care, health and care, enabling students to take as full and active a part as possible in their individual programmes.

During the first year, all students will follow a foundation course, which includes all areas, with the exception of World of Work. In year 2 onwards, students follow individual programmes which will meet their overall assessed needs, as well as the quality assurance requirements of external accreditation, where this is appropriate and of significant relevance to the student.

Links with other establishments

Link courses arranged with Wellingborough College, Northampton College and Moulton College.

Out-of-term contact: Section open 52 weeks of the year, whence information can be obtained, or from: The Shaftesbury Society, 18-20 Kingston Road, South Wimbledon, London SW19 1JZ. Tel: 020 8239 5555, Fax: 020 8239 5580.

Holly Bank School

Roe Head, Far Common Road, Mirfield, West Yorkshire WF14 0DQ
Tel: 01924 490833 Fax: 01924 491464
Email: holly.bank@ukonline.co.uk
Director of Operations: Steven Hughes
Age range: FE 16-19; Rooftops 19-25
Catchment area: Mainly the North of England, but other regions are considered
Controlled by: Governing Body of Holly Bank Trust
Fees: Variable according to needs. Rising annually

Aims to offer excellence in education and development, primarily for children and young adults with complex disabilities.

General description

Building converted to its present use in 1990. School from 5-16, FE department from 16-19. Both departments day and residential. FE accommodation includes three bungalows providing a total of fifteen single bedrooms, each with en-suite facilities. A small number of FE students are accommodated in shared rooms in a flat in the main residential area of the school. All post-16 students meet together at mealtimes and to socialise at various times throughout the day and at evenings and weekends. Rooftops bungalows 19-25 with continued support in accommodation within the community after 25.

Staffing: Teachers; care staff; assistants; physiotherapists; speech therapists; occupational therapists; ICT technicians; nurses; administration; kitchen and maintenance staff. 180 staff employed in total throughout the school and FE department.

Students accepted: 55 students in total, of whom 25 are in FE. All students have physical disabilities and associated profound to moderate learning difficulties. 24 hour nursing cover is available.

Application/selection: Contact the school to arrange a visit, prior to a one-day assessment.

Courses and facilities

Overall ethos is to enable students to move towards self-reliance and greater independence. Individual programmes within a 24 hour curriculum, covering five modules; communication, access and independence, numeracy, mobility, social and community awareness. The ASDAN 'Towards Independence' scheme runs alongside these modules.

Links with other establishments

Links with local further education colleges, training establishments and schools according to individual need.

Out-of-term contact: Limited respite offered for 3 x 5 days during Easter, Spring Bank and Summer Holidays.

Home Farm Trust

Main site: Herald House, 117 Hitchin Road, Shefford,
Bedfordshire SG17 5JD
Tel: 01462 850022 Fax: 01462 850689
Manager: Mrs Irene Livesey
Catchment area: Nationwide   Age range: 19 +
Fees: Approximately £479 to £950 per week

Aims to provide residential and day services for adults with a learning disability.

General description

Opened in autumn 1990, a scheme at the moment for 28 people. The site includes a house for twelve people in which all have their own rooms and where they are encouraged to be responsible for the running of the home and the day service provision; Langford - eight people (Hollycroft); Biggleswade - eight people (Kings Walden Villa). Additional houses in Clifton are near completion; two sets of semi-detached houses, four residents to each semi. One of the houses has been earmarked for people with Prader-Willi Syndrome. The houses are due to open March/April 2000. The Home Farm Trust's approach to care ensures that each resident is regarded as an individual. Thus HFT offers a wide choice of accommodation and activity to its residents whose abilities and needs vary widely.

People accepted: Residents are assessed on an individual basis and the suitability of vacancy.

Applications/selection: Application form from central office in Bristol: Home Farm Trust Ltd, Merchants House, Wapping Road, Bristol BS1 4RQ. Assessment made by Home Farm Trust social worker. Visits to home. Sponsorship agreed.

Courses and facilities

Taking an individual approach to care, the Home Farm Trust offers residents a wide choice of learning and leisure activities. Some are provided in workshops and rooms on the main site.

Links with other establishments

Increasingly, links are being forged with local societies, leisure centres, college and employers, all of whom play an important part in the lives of people with a learning disability.

Out-of-term contact: Open 52 weeks a year.

Homefield College of FE and Vocational Training

42 St. Mary's Road, Sileby, Loughborough, Leicestershire LE12 7TL
Tel: 01509 815696
Principal: Mr. K. O'Brien BSc M.Ed
Catchment area: Nationwide   Age range: 16+
Fees: On application

COPE

Homefield College aims to empower its students to lead an independent life through the provision of a high quality teaching and learning environment which enables them to acquire the independent living, vocational and personal skills which meet their needs and expectations. It provides an adult learning environment in which students can participate in a wide range of activities to enable them to be more independent and self reliant.

General description

The college provides further education and vocational training for 17 young people with learning difficulties. Sileby is a large Midlands village with a full range of community facilities and as such provides a microcosm of town life in which students can learn and gain confidence.

The college is situated in a residential area of the village and is surrounded by neighbours on all sides. We encourage students to participate as fully as possible in the local community and encourage the local community to actively include them. The college curriculum concentrates on the acquisition of key skills, including communication, application of number, working with others, information technology and reviewing own learning. The approach to teaching is cross curricula and delivered across a 24 hour day.

The residential accommodation is organised in such a way as to reinforce the aim of the learning programme. A number of students live in small units within the college which have their own lounge, bathroom and kitchen.

Participation in recreation and leisure activities is given a very high priority and students take part in a wide range of activities in the evenings. As the college is committed to integration and community participation, most social and leisure activities take place in local community facilities rather than specialist segregated settings. The college has a number of houses in the local community, which act as annexes to enable students to practise new skills in a more independent environment.

Staffing: The college has a variety of qualified staff to provide a wide range of programmes. In addition it has the services of a specialist teacher of the hearing impaired and has access to local psychological services when required. Other specialist support services are provided as required.

Students accepted: Students with learning difficulties. The college offers places to students with autistic traits and some behavioural difficulties.

Applications/selection: Completion of a profile/application form. Informal visit with parents/professionals.

Courses and facilities

The college can offer courses of three years duration, designed to meet each student's individual needs. The college is ASDAN and City & Guilds registered and offers a range of courses through 'Towards Independence' as well as Wordpower and Numberpower. The college is able to offer vocational training and work experience to students where appropriate. The college offers NPTC Vocational Foundation Certificate in many vocational areas, and has an allotment, a workshop and access to livery stables. On site courses are complemented by evening classes at the local community college and participation in the Duke of Edinburgh Award Scheme.

Links with other establishments

Links with Loughborough Technical College, Burleigh Community College, The Rathbone Society, Ratcliffe College and Brooksby College of Agriculture.

Out-of-term contact: The college is open 52 weeks a year, with three academic terms.

Honormead School for Children with Autism

Blithbury Road, Blithbury, Rugeley, Staffordshire WS15 3JQ
Tel: 01889 504400 Fax: 01889 504010
Website: www.honormead.btinternet.com
Email: autism@honormead.btinternet.com
Principal: Mrs C Gee
Catchment area: National   Age range: 3-19
Controlled by: Honormead Schools Ltd
Fees: Residential 44 weeks per annum - £60,000; day placement per annum - £42,000

Aims to raise standards further in the education of children with autism through a unique collaboration between Honormead Schools and Boston Higashi School. Aims to allow students to acquire improved levels of emotional stability which will lead to greater opportunity to access the whole curriculum.

General description

Housed in purpose built accommodation, physical education forms the cornerstone of the curriculum. By participating in regular physical education sessions throughout the day, students will disperse excess energy and develop the mental and physical composure to access the whole curriculum. Students are encouraged to learn through an active approach.

Staffing: The staff team is led by the principal and includes a master teacher, class based teachers, head of residence, curriculum care coordinator, educational psychologist, school nurse and classroom and residential assistants.

Students accepted: Day and residential students with autism and associated behavioural disorders.

Application/selection: Application through Statement of Special Educational Needs and subject to satisfactory assessment.

Courses and facilities

The whole school curriculum which includes the National Curriculum is delivered 24 hours a day. Students participate in a varied and stimulating education programme with a strong emphasis on the support of the individual within the group.

The curriculum provides a balance of physical education, academic subjects, independent living skills and creative arts such as art, music and drama.

Links with other establishments

The Boston Higashi School, USA. Parents and local authority professionals.

Ivers

Hains Lane, Marnhull, Sturminster Newton, Dorset DT10 1JU
Tel: 01258 820164 Fax: 01258 820258
Principal: Mr Terence Lane
Catchment area: Unrestricted   Age range: 16-30
Controlled by: Privately owned
Fees: £23,000 to £50,000 dependent on needs

COPE

Aims to meet the needs of young adults and school-leavers with learning difficulties in order that they might be able to move on after two or three years to group or small homes in the community with a considerable degree of independence.

General description

Ivers is a small residential further education establishment for young adults with learning difficulties and/or disabilities. It is registered with Dorset County Council. It provides a homely, caring, personal environment in which young people can mature, develop confidence, learn to relate to other people and acquire skills for life which might enable them to live more independently in the community. The large country house, its extensions, large gardens and paddocks are situated in the village of Marnhull, near Sturminster Newton, between Shaftesbury and Sherborne. Much emphasis is placed upon the acquisition of life skills, which include personal care, laundry, cooking, shopping, money management etc, as well as the continuing development and reinforcement of basic literacy and numeracy skills. All these skills are practised daily, as students learn to be responsible for the tidiness and cleaning of their own rooms and the rest of the house and gardens.

Students accepted: Total of 20. Students with moderate/severe learning difficulties; also those with additional emotional/behavioural problems. Experienced in dealing with epilepsy.

Applications/selection: As much written information as possible, from the local authority, school and family is requested. Past history and care plans are taken into careful consideration. Ivers has a policy of visiting a potential student in his/her own home or school environment to make a brief initial assessment. The student, careers adviser, social worker or parents can then visit us. After consideration, a date can be set for a trial period. A potential student is admitted for approximately one week. During this time he/she is observed carefully, given a wide range of basic tasks and a record is kept of achievement. If this is completed satisfactorily an admission date is set.

Once a student's care and education needs have been determined, a plan is written up. This is carefully monitored and modified, on a regular basis, as necessary. As a student develops and learns in every aspect of his/her life, notes are made by staff on a daily basis. A key-worker takes special responsibility for each student. Monthly tutorial meetings are held with each student and progress is reviewed, setting new targets for the next month.

Reviews are held with the student, parents, social workers and any other concerned professionals every 6 or 12 months, dependent on either need or local authority policy.

Courses and facilities

1. The National Proficiency Tests Council Vocational Foundation Certificate Scheme is used as a framework for all students. The elements levels A and B cover:-

- independent living
- animal care
- horse care
- horticulture
- poultry keeping
- information technology.

2. ASDAN (Award Scheme Development and Accreditation Network) 'Towards Independence' is a programme containing a series of modules which can be undertaken separately and built into a profile of achievement. This is a positive scheme used to plan for individual student's needs.

Jacques Hall Foundation

Harwich Road, Bradfield, Manningtree, Essex CO11 2XW
Tel: 01255 870311 Fax: 01225 870377
Email: principal@jacques-hall.co.uk
Principal: Mr T Rodwell
Catchment area: Nationwide   Age range: 11-18
Controlled by: Jacques Hall Foundation
Fees: On application

A therapeutic community for emotionally damaged adolescents in which they can feel safe and secure to explore their difficulties, to cope with their anger, create change and therefore lead more fulfilling lives in the future.

General description

Rural setting in North Essex, including 16 acres of land with 19th century country house. Additional buildings include school, art studio, workshops, vegetable gardens, animal houses and semi-independence unit.

Staffing: Three senior managers; three team leaders; nine community workers, eight support workers; seven teachers including one senior; one classroom assistant; six ancillary staff; five administrative staff; one admissions and marketing officer; one consultant child and adolescent psychiatrist; one educational psychologist; one art therapist.

Students accepted: A total of 26, mixed.

Applications/selection: Following receipt of all appropriate reports, social worker and family to visit followed by interview of child in current placement, after which child visits for a day. Process takes one month - initial placement for 28 day assessment period.

Courses and facilities

In addition to the community's own full education programme, still being made available to post-16 youngsters, work experience and social skills programmes are offered both with Jacques Hall and within the local community.

Links with other establishments

Involvement with various local colleges.

Landmarks

Upper Mill Farm, Creswell, Worksop, Nottinghamshire S80 4HP
Tel: 01909 724724 Fax: 01909 724725
Website: www.creswell.co.uk/landmarks/
Email: info@landmarks.creswell.co.uk
Principal: Damian Prior   Age Range: 16 +
Catchment area: Nottinghamshire/Derbyshire/South Yorkshire

COPE

Personal programmes and learning activities are designed to provide each participant with the best opportunity to develop their skills and potential and to equip them for a positive role in their community.

General description

Landmarks provides a safe, caring and stimulating environment for people with learning difficulties and disabilities.

Nestling in a prehistoric gorge shared with the famous Ice Age settlement of Creswell Crags, Landmarks is based on a traditional working farm and on a site of outstanding natural beauty on the Nottinghamshire/Derbyshire border.

Purpose built facilities are designed to provide a high standard of accommodation for work and study and to allow access to people with physical and mobility problems.

Programmes are designed around seasonal and annual cycles and provide people with all the benefits which arise from increased self awareness, self confidence and awareness of the needs of others.

Staffing: Landmarks staff are chosen for their exceptional personal qualities, their professional experience, qualifications and attitude and understanding of the special needs of people whom we work with. Students have their own personal tutor who takes a special interest in their progress and development and helps with any problems or frustrations.

The level of support provided is agreed through inter-agency reviews and our comprehensive Initial Assessment and it is continuously monitored. Normal working group size is around 6, allowing a high degree of personal support and attention.

Application/selection: Application is by letter, phone or email, in the first instance to the Programmes Manager, at the above address. Selection is on the basis of student need and the outcome of a selection process based on a series of taster days and work experiences. Currently only day provision is offered, but residential provision is planned.

Courses and facilities

Landmarks offers a range of courses in pottery and traditional crafts, especially dried flower gardening, animal care and a range of practical land-based activities related to the running of the farm. All the courses are accredited with either the OCN or the NPTC.

Operating since 1995, Landmarks has developed a range of facilities and resources, specifically for the use of people with disabilities. The following are amongst the resources available: fully equipped ceramics workshop, general craft workshop, farm maintenance workshop, fully equipped kitchen, large working farm with range of new and traditional farm buildings, milking parlour and dairy, farm equipment, with modern and traditional tools, farm and domestic animals, poultry unit and aviary, gardens, greenhouse and equipment, classrooms and libraries complete with video and IT equipment, conservation area with tree nursery planned.

Links with other establishments

Landmarks is an independent charity but operates in close partnership with other local providers of services for people with learning difficulties and disabilities. In particular, it has collaborative arrangements with several local FE colleges which optimises the opportunities for people to ultimately move on to further/mainstream education or training.

Larchfield Community

Stokesley Road, Hemlington, Middlesbrough TS8 9DY
Tel: 01642 593688/595143 Fax: 01642 595778
Website: www.camphill.org.uk
Principal: Community run through groups responsible for each area of work
Age range: 21 +
Catchment area: 1. Middlesbrough area 2. Nationwide
Controlled by: Camphill Village Trust Communities. (Registered office: 19 South Road, Stourbridge DY8 3YA)
Fees: Local authority - which includes state benefits

Working urban fringe community first initiated between Middlesbrough Council and Camphill Village Trust. Training schemes for people with learning difficulties.

General description

Larchfield is a land-based community on the southern fringe of Middlesbrough where ultimately 60 people will live and work together in a therapeutic community based around market gardening, farming, food processing and craft work.

Staffing: Co-workers as part of the community.

Students accepted: Adults from 21 years seem to find the environment at Larchfield the best challenge.

Applications/selection: Clinic for residential placements. Local (Middlesbrough) Social Services department for day placements.

Courses and facilities

- Larchfield Foods - butchery and food processing.
- Larchfield Bakery - production bakery.
- Wheelhouse Coffee Bar - volunteers manning coffee bar in mornings for community
- woodwork shop
- weavery

Training places available in -

- car mechanic workshop
- catering workshop.

Farming and horticulture provide the community with a varied workload as there is much to do to develop the land into a properly working bio-dynamic farm, as well as market and kitchen gardens.

Links with other establishments

With Middlesbrough Borough Council, and Council for Voluntary Service, Middlesbrough Social Services and Camphill Communities. North Yorkshire Social Services and other social services departments.

Lindeth College

The Oaks, Lindeth, Bowness-on-Windermere, Cumbria LA23 3NH
Tel: 015394 46265 Fax: 015394 88840
Principal: Lawrence Mannion
Catchment area: Nationwide   Age range: 16-25
Controlled by: Lindeth College
Fees: On application

COPE

Lindeth College is a specialist residential further education college for students with learning difficulties and disabilities.

General description

A seven acre campus comprising a main building, a new office and education building and six training houses.

Staffing: 27 full-time staff including a qualified nurse.

Students accepted: 44 residential students; no day students.

Applications/selection: Direct to the college. Students attend an initial interview and a trial week as part of the application procedure.

Courses and facilities

Individual learning programmes are based on independent living skills, literacy and numeracy and vocational skills. The latter includes internal and external work placements, horticulture, woodwork and workshop practice and building maintenance.

Students work towards external accreditation if possible, using NPTC, RSA, and Wordpower/Numberpower schemes.

Students normally attend Lindeth College for a three-year course, moving from the main building to independent training houses as the course progresses.

The focus for all students is independent living skills which are promoted through the extended curriculum in addition to the formal curriculum. The college has an evening and weekend leisure programme which students are encouraged to participate in. A high level of staff support exists throughout the curriculum.

Links with other establishments

We are members of both ARC (Association of Residential Communities) and NATSPEC (National Association of Specialist Colleges). We are inspected by both the Further Education Funding Council and Social Services.

Linkage Specialist FE College

Weelsby Campus, Grimsby, NE Lancs DN32 9RU
Tel: 01472 361334 Fax: 01472 242375
Chief Executive: Dr Bob Price Education Director: Jean Blakeley
Age Range: 16 +
Catchment area: Unrestricted, including overseas
Controlled by: Linkage Community Trust (Registered Charity)
Fees: Individually determined

The college aims to create a stimulating environment based on a curriculum which provides academic, vocational and social development for young adults with learning difficulties and other disabilities. The college supports every student in working towards realising his/her full potential for independence and a happy and fulfilling life.

General description

The college is made up of three campuses all of which are located within the old county of Lincolnshire. Toynton Campus is situated in a rural setting one mile from the market town of Spilsby. Weelsby Campus is set in gardens and woodlands but is only minutes from the centre of the town of Grimsby and the neighbouring seaside resort of Cleethorpes. Both provide student accommodation of a high standard within their respective main halls and in the many Linkage owned houses within the local communities. Sampson Campus lies on the outskirts of the city of Lincoln and accommodates 18 students. This facility provides a further challenge to those students who have developed their independence skills at either Toynton or Weelsby.

The college works closely with each student's family/carers, careers officer and other professionals in reviewing the student's progress and planning for the future. Students are encouraged to keep in regular contact with their home area and family through regular weekends home during term time. There is a dedicated team of staff who work with the home area careers officer, family and social worker to ensure suitable provision is available to enable all students to progress further when their course at Linkage College has come to a close.

Quality: Linkage College has achieved National Record of Achievement Validation, Basic Skills Agency (Quality Standard) and Investor in People status.

Staffing: The college has a generous complement of professional, specialist and experienced staff. Linkage's Staff Development Team ensures the continuous professional development of all staff members. Each student is allocated a personal tutor.

Students accepted: Linkage College has 218 places in total and provides for males and females. The college is able to consider applications from young people with moderate or severe learning difficulties, Downs syndrome, speech and language difficulties, autism, Asperger's syndrome, visual and hearing impairments, epilepsy, William's syndrome and other physical disabilities.

Applications: Forms are available from the college admissions department on 01472 361334.

Courses and facilities

All students have individually planned courses which are regularly monitored. The course duration is of either two or three years. Courses generally begin at the start of the autumn term, although occasionally places are available to start in January or April. Courses include basic education and independence, vocational education, and there is a comprehensive and progressive programme aimed at developing social and independent living skills.

Links with other establishments

There is a strong emphasis on the integration of students into the community and local facilities, including sports and recreational provision, social and entertainment venues and local colleges are accessed fully by Linkage college students.

Living Options (Formerly the CRYPT Foundation)

Kimbridge House, Kimbridge Road, East Wittering, Chichester, W. Sussex PO20 8PE

Tel: 01243 671865

Chairman: Mrs V C Fethney

Catchment area: National

Age range: 18-30

Controlled by: Executive committee and local management committees

Fees: From April £560 per week

Aims to provide opportunities for young people with physical disabilities to live in small group homes in the community.

General description

'Gavarnie', Brackensham is an adapted bungalow. Students attend local colleges of FE and receive in-house tuition. Kimbridge House is a large adapted house for students and carers. New project Fennes for a further four persons.

Staffing: Young CSV care staff; driver; project coordinator oversees the project.

Students accepted: Brackensham, West Sussex can take students with physical disabilities, either sex.

Applications/selection: Application is followed by an informal visit which in turn is followed by an interview and assessment.

Courses and facilities

Impossible to list. Prospectus available from: Earnley Concourse, Chichester Adult Education Department. Duration ranges from four-day continuous to weekend continuous to once weekly, throughout the year. All students work on individual programmes, if required.

Links with other establishments

Depends on courses students wish to study.

The Loddon School

Wildmoor, Sherfield-on-Loddon, Hook, Hants RG27 0JD
Tel: 01256 882394 Fax: 01256 882929
Principal: Mrs Marion Cornick
Age range: 8-19
Catchment area: London and Home Counties preferred
Controlled by: The Loddon School Trust
Fees: Dependent on need

Aims to provide education for children with severe learning difficulties and challenging behaviour, and autism.

General description

The school is situated five miles from Basingstoke in a Victorian country home. Children have single or shared bedrooms, and live in one of two individually staffed units on a family basis. The school concentrates also on communication, relationship building and the functional lifeskills curriculum.

Staffing: The school employs more than 140 staff including 1:1 ratio in most situations.

Students accepted: 27 places. Must be 16 or younger on admission.

Applications/selection: Application forms and questionnaires from Principal. Visits by school staff to assess child; followed by visits from parents. Transition programmes planned following acceptance.

Courses and facilities

The school specialises in children with the most severe learning difficulties and autism. Our curriculum uses a mixture of behavioural work and gentle teaching, with an emphasis on reward for positive behaviours. Music, massage and sensory work are important features and are used to facilitate communication, reduce stress, and encourage relationship-building.

Links with other establishments

Parent courses and opportunities for parents to stay in the school are helpful for families and ensure continuity of management and consistency of approach. Liaise Loddon Ltd is developing houses in the community for school-leavers who present severe problems usually associated with autism. Details available from Loddon School.

Out-of-term contact: Open 52 weeks a year.

Longdon Hall School

Longdon Green, Rugeley, Staffordshire WS15 4PT
Tel: 01543 490634 Fax: 01543 492140
Website: www.honormead.btinternet.com
Email: longdonhallschool@honormead.btinternet.com
Principal: Mrs C Georgeson
Catchment area: National   Age ranges: 5-19
Controlled by: Honormead Schools Ltd
Fees per term: Boarding - £13,260; day - £7,960; 50 week boarding - £15,630; 52 week boarding - £16,350 (Additional fees for special care)

The school's aims are: to reflect education, care and language and communication therapy in the whole school curriculum; to present a safe, happy, and welcoming environment; to provide creative and imaginative teaching through meaningful activities and settings; to promote the physical, intellectual, cultural, moral and spiritual development of all pupils to meet personal and social goals in the wider community.

General description

Longdon Hall school is a centre of excellence in meeting the needs of pupils who have a combination of communication and learning difficulties, which would best be met by an extensive and holistic approach including TEACCH (Treatment and Education of Autistic and Related Communication Handicapped Children).

Staffing: Includes teachers, clinical and educational psychologists, speech and language therapists, occupational therapist, physiotherapist, riding therapists, nurses and student support staff.

Students accepted: Day and residential placements for pupils with a combination of communication and learning difficulties and autism.

Application/selection: Application through Statement of Special Educational Needs and subject to satisfactory assessment.

Courses and facilities

Access to National Curriculum, assessment and external accreditation and examinations. Academic and vocational education, careers guidance and work experience. Community and work-based activities. Enhanced independence and personal responsibility, spiritual, moral and cultural development.

Links with other establishments

Links with mainstream schools and FE colleges. Post-16 provision at Eastfields FE centre, part of Longdon Hall School. Post-19 provision currently being developed by the school. Parents and local authority professionals, Green Laud, FE centre.

Loppington House

Further Education Unit and Adult Centre, Loppington, Nr. Wem, Shropshire SY4 5NF
Tel: 01939 233926 Fax: 01939 235255
Manager: P. Harris
Catchment area: Nationwide   Age range: 16 +
Controlled by: Plc (registered with Shropshire Social Services under the Registered Care Homes Act of 1984)
Fees: available on application

Aims to offer each student the opportunity to develop a positive approach to life, with high staffing ratios and professional support.

General description

FEFC Grade 2 listed by the Further Education Funding Council.

A residential care home situated in a parkland setting in North Shropshire close to the market town of Wem and 14 miles from the county town of Shrewsbury. It is divided into five residential units and four training areas. The young people are given the opportunity to develop their academic and social skills to their fullest potential, thus enabling them to lead a more independent lifestyle.

Staffing: 21 education centre staff; 34 care staff; ten night supervisors; one nurse; five administration staff; four kitchen staff; eight domestic assistants and two maintenance staff.

Students accepted: Young men and women who have severe learning difficulties and associated behavioural problems.

Application/selection: By application to the Manager in the first instance.

Courses and facilities

Education centre divided into four groups:

- adult literacy and numeracy
- art and craft
- social skills
- rural studies.

Loppington House is a member of the Riding for the Disabled Association and all students are given the opportunity of riding ponies and driving in the pony and trap.

'The Poplars', a residential unit for eight young adults over the age of 21, puts the emphasis on social and independence training where each student is allocated their own personal programme according to their ability.

We have developed community links initially with a workshop based on the local town giving our young adults the opportunity to work and experience a high degree of public interaction. We also have a retail shop in the local town, which has broadened the opportunities for community links.

Links with other establishments

North Shropshire College; Telford College of Arts and Technology; Oswestry College.

Lord Mayor Treloar National Specialist College

Holybourne, Alton, Hants GU34 4EN
Tel: 01420 547425 Fax: 01420 542708
Email: admissions@treloar.org.uk
Principal: G K Jowett PhD, MSc, BSc, CQSW, Cert Ed (FE)
Catchment area: Nationwide (regional bias)   Age range: 16-25
Controlled by: Treloar Trust

COPE

The college strives for excellence in education, therapy and care in an environment which encourages young people with disabilities to achieve their potential. Most students proceed to integrated further or higher education, open or supported employment and enhanced independent living skills.

General description

Situated close to Alton, within easy reach of London, the college caters for up to 172 students. Comprehensive care including night cover. Rehabilitation Engineering Department. Daily or residential status. A swimming pool, a gymnasium, a wheelchair race track, Polygym. Close cooperation with local Sports Centres and groups. Riding, sailing, Duke of Edinburgh Award Scheme, Scouts, Guides etc.

Staffing: 25 full-time & 7 part-time teachers; 21 teaching assistants; 10 support workers; 3 full-time & 16 part-time medical care staff; 33 full-time & 73 part-time house care staff; 5 full-time & 1 part-time physiotherapists; 4 full-time & 3 part-time occupational therapists and extended curriculum manager; 2 full-time & 3 part-time speech therapists; 1 full-time driving instructor; a medical officer who is also a local GP, dietician, educational psychologist, counselling team, specialist careers guidance service, work experience coordinator, activities organiser.

Students accepted: Physical disabilities with associated sensory or cognitive impairment, but not totally blind or deaf. Academic range from learning difficulties to university entrance. Nursing care and medical needs and complex care needs can be catered for. Waking night cover. Age range 16-25 years (also 5-16 years on a separate site). Present numbers 70 female and 113 male aged 16+.

Applications/selection: No entry examination. Potential candidates and parents visit on Tuesdays during term time. Selection by interview/assessment by multidisciplinary team. Applications accepted at any time if appropriate provision can be made. Intakes usually September but occasionally at other times. Most funded by FEFC.

Courses and facilities

General education GCSE (mature); A levels, Advanced GNVQs taken in conjunction with Alton Tertiary College.

A wide range of vocational courses leading to certification as appropriate for individuals and including City & Guilds, GCSE, RSA, Pitmans, AEB Basic Skills, GNVQs and NVQs, EdExcel and ASDAN Award Scheme.

The vocational skills centre (the Traill Centre) has specialist facilities for all vocational courses including photographic, media studies and new music recording studio; new horticulture centre, computer rooms; and new Learning Resources Centre. Independence training flats and large therapy department; specialist help for specific learning difficulties and support teaching for individuals; group and individual counselling.

Links with other establishments

Staff/student exchange with Alton Tertiary College, especially A level and Advanced GNVQs, and other colleges. Duke of Edinburgh Award Scheme linked with local schools and also certain sporting activities. Adult education integrated on college campus.

The Lothlorien Community Ltd

Woodend, Cannongate Road, Hythe, Kent CT21 5PX
Tel: 01303 230131 Fax: 01303 230145
Website: www.lothlorien.co.uk
Email: info@lothlorien.co.uk
Director of Care: Mrs Yvonne Wantstall
Head of Care: Mrs Penny Excell
Catchment area: Nationwide   Age range: 18 +
Fees: Negotiable according to level of support need

Aims to empower and enable disabled people to live as equal members of society through the provision of community-based homes and an extensive further development programme.

General description

The community currently runs eight different homes within normal community settings in the Hythe and Folkestone area. All residents enjoy individual rooms and each person is encouraged to personalise that room according to their wishes. The basis for the support provided is respect for people as individuals. Each person's programme of development is based on their individual need.

Students accepted: Students must be 18+ but some pre-18 assessment work can be considered. Individual assessment takes place, complex medical needs can be catered for, e.g. uncontrolled epilepsy, diabetes, Prader-Willi syndrome etc. People with autism are also numbered amongst the current group of residents. The community is registered with The National Autistic Society and is working towards full accreditation as a recognised provider of appropriate services for people with autism.

Application/selection: Contact should be made through either the Director or Head of Care.

Courses and facilities

A considerable range of workshop and classroom activities takes place on the Woodend site. Opportunities are also sought for community-based work experience.

Links with other establishments

Close links are in place with the nearby Adult Education College and courses available cover a wide spectrum. Currently, students are pursuing both NVQ and City & Guilds qualifications. Less able students are also pursuing vocational courses. All ability levels can be catered for.

Open 52 weeks a year

Love Walk Residential Care Home

10 Love Walk, Denmark Hill, London SE5 8AE
Tel: 020 7703 3632 Fax: 020 7252 4958
Head of Home: To be appointed
Age range: 18 +
Catchment area: Unrestricted
Controlled by: Mission Care Trustees
Fees: £490 single, £350 shared, per week

Aims to provide a home and high standard of care, for physically disabled people, encouraging independence and autonomy.

General description

Easy access to central London and close to public transport, local shops etc: en suite single flatlets with facilities for making snacks. Dining room, sitting room, leisure room, utility rooms for use of residents. Garaging for light vehicles and wheelchairs. Sometimes only shared flatlets available.

Staffing: Day and night care.

Clients accepted: Most physical disabilities represented.

Applications/selection: Details from the Manager.

Courses and facilities

Tuition available in typewriting, art, craft, keep fit, dressmaking.

Links with other establishments

Further education tutors on site as above. Wheelchair accessible courses available at local colleges of FE & AEI.

Out-of-term contact: Open all year round.

Lufton Manor College

Lufton, Yeovil, Somerset BA22 8ST
Tel: 01935 423124
Principal: Margaret Reader
Age range: 16-25
Catchment area: Nationwide
Controlled by: MENCAP

Provides further education and training to support the transition to adulthood.

General description

Two sites on the rural outskirts of Yeovil, with extensive grounds, including a farm, woodland, gardens, glasshouses and a café open to the public. Accommodation ranges from sheltered to self-catering.

Courses and facilities

Community facilities in Yeovil ensure a range of leisure activities are available. All students register with a local GP.

Staffing: 64 staff.

Students accepted: Students with moderate/severe learning difficulties. 70 students, mixed. Specialist provision for students with communication difficulties.

Applications/selection: Forms available from the Principal, informal visits welcome. Full 5 day residential interview/assessment period.

Links with other establishments

Students enrol at any time for a two- or three-year course. Following an induction and initial assessment period, an individual learning programme is produced, covering vocational training and employability, independence skills, personal care and daily living, basic skills and decision-making/problem-solving. Students can work in any of the following vocational areas: farming, hotel and catering, office skills, horticulture, grounds maintenance and craft/retail.

All courses are accredited internally and are designed to lead on to NVQ level 1 which is also available at the college in a number of vocational areas. All students receive a Record of Achievement. Students develop functional skills in literacy and numeracy to support everyday living and vocational areas. As students progress, opportunities of work experience placements in the community, and part-time courses at Yeovil College, are available. A Mencap Pathways officer works at the college to link these experiences in with future placements on leaving college.

MacIntyre Care

602 South Seventh Street, Milton Keynes, Buckinghamshire
MK9 2JA
Tel: 01908 230100 Fax: 01908 695643
Managing Director: Bill Mumford
Catchment area: England and Wales   Age range: 8 +
Controlled by: Registered charity
Fees: They differ for each project or unit according to resources

Aims to provide the best possible service for people with learning difficulties, based on individual need and aspirations.

General description

Provides a wide range of services across the UK, including two residential schools, community-based residential support, day services and training opportunities and supported living schemes.

Staffing: Levels in each service vary according to the level of support service users require.

Students accepted: People with a learning disability, autism, epilepsy, challenging behaviour and communication difficulties.

Applications/selection: For more detailed information about the range of provision and details of vacancies contact Clare Campling at Centre Office.

Mary Hare Grammer School for the Deaf

Arlington Manor, Snelsmore Common, Newbury, Berkshire RG14 3BQ

Tel: 01635 244200 Minicom: 01635 244260

Fax: 01635 248019

Website: www.maryhare.org.uk

Principal: I G Tucker PhD

Catchment area: National and international   Age range: 11-19

Controlled by: Mary Hare Schools

Fees: Paid in full by LEA or FEFC £19,160 (99/00)

Aims to offer a broad curriculum to severely and profoundly hearing-impaired children, enabling them to pursue courses to GCSE, A level and a range of Advanced GNVQs. The Sixth Form at Mary Hare is built upon the belief that deaf young people are just as capable as their hearing counterparts. At the same time, we acknowledge that deafness can be a significant disability and we seek to provide an environment where that barrier can be overcome. Our teaching staff are specialist teachers of the deaf who are also specialist subject teachers. Groups are small - rarely larger than six or seven - and there is great scope for individual help and support. We believe that students do best if they are taught through spoken language and for this reason sign language is not used. We pay great attention to the amplification needs of our students and also to the layout and design of our classrooms which are all acoustically treated.

General description

The school has excellent facilities, 140 acre site, six science laboratories, large library, excellent sporting facilities, design technology suite, computer suites, open access computer rooms for students, media studies facility, large hall, swimming pools etc.

A 66 bedroom sixth form centre, the Wroughton Centre, was officially opened by HRH Princess Margaret, Countess of Snowdon, in May 1995.

Staffing: 66 teachers in specialist subject areas who are also teachers of the deaf; two nurses; 33 care staff - three large boarding houses each with Head of House.

Students accepted: 210 hearing-impaired children of above average ability. Co-educational. Entry is possible age 16+ subject to GCSE results.

Applications/selection: Places are offered following an annual entrance examination in November. Interviews are held in December when the children undertake further tests. Headteachers' reports and local authority recommendations are taken into consideration. Notification of results to headteachers and local education authorities by Christmas.

Courses and facilities

All major courses to GCSE and A level - National Curriculum.

Advanced GNVQs in art and design, business and finance, and media studies.

GCSE - art and design, biology, business studies, CDT, chemistry, child development, computer studies, design and communication, electronics, English, food, French studies, French, geography, history, home economics, human biology, maths, media studies, physics, religious studies and textiles.

A level - art, biology, chemistry, English literature, French, geography, graphics, history, maths, physics, sociology and textiles. Also AS level subjects.

Links with other establishments

Close links with Newbury College of FE for students to take enrichment courses, e.g. computer-aided design, typing, and full academic courses for A levels/BTEC.

Out-of-term contact: School office staffed apart from public holidays. Brochures and videos available on request.

Meldreth Manor School

Fenny Lane, Meldreth, Royston, Hertfordshire SG8 6LG
Tel: 01763 260771 Fax: 01763 263316
Head teacher: David Banes
Catchment area: No restrictions   Age range: 5-19
Controlled by: SCOPE
Fees: Full board £48,176 pa; weekly boarding £43,360 pa; day £30,352 pa

Aims to provide for the specialised educational requirements of young people with physical disabilities and severe or profound learning difficulties.

General description

Purpose-built and resourced school situated in the village of Meldreth, three miles from Royston, eleven miles from Cambridge. Development of supported living in a range of residential accommodation.

Staffing: Teachers, physiotherapists, occupational therapist, speech therapists, nursing staff and support workers. Additional support including music and dance/movement.

Students accepted: Provides an education for pupils with physical disabilities and severe or profound learning difficulties. The school caters for pupils with additional sensory impairments and medical needs.

Applications/selection: Informal visits welcomed. Assessment for placement arranged on request.

Courses and facilities

Meldreth Manor School has a commitment to provide an education which is supportive of each pupil's individual needs within a caring and stimulating environment. In order to fulfil this aim, the school, through a considered and balanced 24 hour curriculum, provides a high standard of education and social care with an emphasis upon personal dignity and self-esteem for all pupils.

Links with other establishments

Meldreth Manor School has established good links with several mainstream schools and colleges with whom activities are often shared. The importance of leisure and recreation is given a high priority, pupils attending youth clubs, Scouts, Guides etc. in the local area.

Out-of-term-contact: Head teacher's secretary at the school.

The Mental Health Care Group

Head Office, Alexander House, Highfield Park, Llandyrnog,
Denbigh, Denbighshire LL16 4LU
Tel: 01824 790600 Fax: 01824 790727
Home manager: Clive Jones
Catchment area: Nationwide   Age range: Adults
Controlled by: The Mental Health Care Group

tHEMental Health Care Group offers a full range of services along a continuum of care which stretches from highly staffed mental nursing , through residential care to supported tenancies. The Group, which has 170 registered beds, services people who are difficult to place, both with learning disabilities and/or mental health problems.

General description

Application/selection: By contacting our Head Office your enquiries and referrals will be given to our strategic support team which will assess service users in conjunction with their own social workers to find the most appropriate placement within the Group. We have a range of services which are provided separately for people who have learning disabilities, mental health problems, difficulties which cross client group boundaries, and people with forensic backgrounds.

- Assessment
- A range of nursing, residential and support services
- A strategic multidisciplinary support team
- Full-time forensic clinical psychologist
- Full-time consultant psychiatrist
- Quality assurance inspection to ISO 9002
- Institute of Health and Care Development accredited NVQ assessment centre
- Investor in People
- Detained bed status under the Mental Health Act 1983 at New Hall Mental Nursing Home
- CCETSW approved social work agency

Courses and facilities

Our response to the needs of every resident for education, training and work is tailored individually and kept under review. This calls for a very wide range of activities and staff to match, and to support this we have a development plan, with both short and long term goals, aimed at the progressive development of all our residents. Our work experience programme is notably successful, expanding and undergoing fine tuning for the individuals involved. The placements consists of work situations both on and off site.

Links with other establishments

Interchange has commenced with Llanrillo College of Further Education, Colwyn Bay. In-service courses at Cartrefle College are encouraged and supported.

Minstead Training Project

Minstead Lodge, Minstead, Nr. Lyndhurst, Hants SO43 7FT
Tel: 01703 812254 Fax: 01703 812297
Principal: Martin Lenaerts
Age range: 16-30
Controlled by: Peter Selwood Charitable Trust
Catchment area: Nationwide
Fees: Residential from £280.00 per week (includes DSS payment). Day from £115.00 per week. Reviewed annually

Aims to offer our students, who have learning disabilities, training in work, life and social skills leading to greater maturity and independence.

General description

Large country house set in 17 acres of land comprising fields, ornamental and kitchen gardens, greenhouse and workshops, with a further eight acres close by comprising public garden/nursery and sales area. A variety of leisure pursuits are arranged both on site and outside with students encouraged to choose preferred leisure pursuits and activities.

Staffing: Principal: six instructors; one teacher; eight full-time and four part-time care staff; secretary and input from selected volunteers.

Students accepted: Those with learning disabilities. 13 residential students male/female. Day students also accepted. Longer term care, minimal supervision and sheltered work are offered as a step on as appropriate and when available.

Applications/selection: Initial informal visit. Application. Funding arranged. Short trial stay. Final decision.

Courses and facilities

Initially a two-year course, but the needs of the individual student are taken into account near the end of this period and there is no automatic cut off, although it is envisaged that all students move on at an appropriate time to appropriate living and working/occupational settings. Students have 15 working days leave per year, plus the time between Christmas and New Year when the project is closed.

The course is geared mainly towards practical skills, with the work skills covering all aspects of horticulture. Some students work alongside our catering staff at times and there is a wood and craft workshop. Those who have the aptitude are encouraged to take up work experience opportunities and/or places at local colleges where courses tie in with their particular abilities and interests.

Qualifications offered on site are NPTC horticulture, NPTC workshop practice, NPTC independent living skills, NVQ amenity horticulture and OCR National Skills Profile and IT skills.

Domestic skills training covers all aspects of everyday home life and students are expected to learn the necessary skills to look after their part of the house. The accommodation is split into five flats with differing levels of independence in order that students can make steady progress.

Consumer skills are taught, covering the areas of shopping, use of money, public transport, etc. In all aspects of training, staff input is given to the level each individual requires but always with an eye to stepping back and allowing a person to go it alone.

There is also plenty of scope for help in the areas of social skills and character development. Each student also spends some time each week on literacy and numeracy. The project has a five-resident longer-term house in the village. For those requiring greater independence there are three minimally-staffed houses in nearby towns.

A sheltered work scheme in contract gardening is available offering a real work environment in off site contracts with staff support.

Links with other establishments

No specific links. All links are made as and when appropriate with organisations such as local colleges.

Motherwell College

Dalzell Drive, Motherwell, Lanarkshire ML1 2DD
Tel: 01698 232323 Fax: 01698 275430
E-mail: mcol@motherwell.co.uk
Principal and Chief Executive: Richard Millham
Catchment area: No restrictions   Age range: 16-60
Fees: Depends on level and duration of course

Motherwell College is a community college providing further education to individuals of all ages and abilities, both locally and nationally, through choice of courses at advanced and non-advanced levels.

General description

Motherwell College is within easy reach of the town centre, which has excellent transport links by bus and rail to the rest of Scotland. It is minutes away from Strathclyde Park which has facilities for a variety of leisure pursuits. The College provides easy access for disabled students by means of ramps and lifts. Stewart Hall of Residence is situated on the campus and provides accommodation for 46 students.

Students accepted: Motherwell College provides for some 16,000 students between the age of 16 and 60. In addition to our mainstream courses, the college provides full-time/part-time, day-release/link and evening classes for students who are physically disabled, sensory impaired, communication impaired and those with learning difficulties from schools, adult training centres and hospitals both locally and nationally.

Applications/selection: Applications for courses are made by individuals or through careers officers, social workers, psychologists, voluntary agencies and schools. Future needs assessments help to determine the individual's ability to participate in and benefit from the college's wide range of provision.

Courses and facilities

The college offers a range of courses, both full-time and part-time, to meet the needs of physically disabled, blind and visually impaired, deaf and hearing impaired, communication impaired, stroke and accident victims and large number of young people and adults with learning difficulties. Education is provided on an outreach basis to approximately 400 people from adult training centres, hospitals and voluntary organisations.

The college policy is one of integration. Students may be accepted by any team within the college with support available from the specialist staff or learning support staff.

Links with other establishments

The college has strong links with other agencies including: social work department, careers service, psychological services, RNIB, RNID, schools for the physically disabled, Scottish Centre for the Disabled, Scottish Council on Disability, Scottish Council for Education Technology, CALL Centre, special schools, health boards and voluntary organisations. The college is also the Scottish coordinating centre for the National Federation of Access Centres.

Contact: Irvine Kinghorn, Curriculum leader, Support for Learning; Jeanette Gillies, Curriculum leader, Personal and Social Development

The Mount Camphill Community

Faircrouch Lane, Wadhurst, East Sussex TN5 6PT
Tel: 01892 782025 Fax: 01892 782917
Website: www.camphill.org.uk
Email: themount@camphill.ndirect.co.uk

Age range: 16-25
Catchment area: Principally South and East England
Controlled by: Member of Association of Camphill Communities
Fees: £19,750 per annum - 4 term year (38 weeks approx.)

Aims to provide education, training and community living for adolescents and young adults in need of special understanding in such a way that the full potential of each member of the community is developed to the full.

General description

The Community consists of approximately 60 individuals including teachers, craft teachers and other co-workers. The estate comprises approximately 20 acres of pasture and woodland and includes a two acre walled garden and orchard. Students are accommodated in four houses. The main building was formerly a Victorian monastery; in addition there are two houses where a more family type atmosphere prevails and a fourth house which provides the opportunity for more independent living. In addition to the daily life, there is a rich artistic and cultural life within the community built around the celebration of the Christian festivals.

Staffing: Co-workers and students live together in family units, sharing responsibility for the management and upkeep of the houses. Resident co-workers trained in curative education, youth guidance and social therapy work together with younger resident co-workers. Other specialist teachers and therapists work on a daily basis.

Students accepted: The Mount accepts students with a wide range of learning difficulties and emotional disturbances. Some day places are available. Students are admitted from the age of 16 to Foundation Course, to complete their pre-college education, and from the age of 18 to the college.

Applications/selection: Please telephone for a brochure or write to The Admissions Group giving a brief description of your enquiry. We like to see a recent report on a student before offering an interview. It is possible for social workers and/or parents to visit without the student, prior to making an application. If everyone, including the student, agrees that a placement at The Mount is appropriate, a place will be offered with the first term treated as a trial period.

Courses and facilities

Pupils aged between 16 and 18 receive a full creative schooling based on the Waldorf curriculum of Rudolf Steiner. Subjects include literacy, numeracy, science, social skills, eurythmy, gymnastics, drama and music as well as craft activities. From the age of 18 students are admitted to the college where they specialise in a particular craft or work area which they choose from the options available: baking, woodwork, horticulture, pottery, weaving and cooking and catering. Students are encouraged to experience a number of workshops at the beginning of their course before making a choice. Some City & Guilds courses are followed; individual tuition is given in literacy and numeracy where appropriate. In their final year of college, the students spend three or four weeks in another Camphill Community developing their work skills in a different environment. The facilities also include a sports hall and an area for outside games.

Students may remain at The Mount after the end of their college period to consolidate their skills. They take a more active part in the work of the community as part of their reparation for the transition to adult life.

Links with other establishments

The Mount works closely with other Camphill Rudolf Steiner Communities and has a number of links with other educational establishments in Kent and East Sussex. There is an active relationship with the local secondary school.

Out-of-term-contact: As many of the co-workers make their home in the community there is normally a contact available at all times.

Nash College of Further Education

Coney Hill Education Centre, Croydon Road, Hayes, Bromley, Kent BR2 7AG

Tel: 020 8462 7419 Fax: 020 8462 0347

Principal: Karen Fletcher-Wright MEd

Catchment area: Nationwide

Age range: 16-25

Controlled by: The Shaftesbury Society

Fees: On request

Aims to provide high quality education and training to young people with physical and learning disabilities.

General description

Nash College of Further Education is a residential college for young people. Most of our students are funded by the FEFC with help from their Social Services departments. We are situated in a lovely wooded site but very close to Bromley for shopping trips and only 30 minutes from Central London. Whilst most residential students live on site there is an opportunity for progression to living in the community. Our courses range from independence skills to City and Guilds courses and we can cater for the whole range of physical and learning disabilities provided that we feel they can benefit from what we have to offer. Amongst the many subjects on offer are horticulture, business studies, catering and art. We also specialise in teaching young people with no speech to use voice output communication aids. We have excellent up-to-date computer facilities.

Staffing: A multi-disciplinary team of teachers, classroom assistants, technicians, nurses, therapists, counsellors and carers. We have a visiting GP, medical consultants, orthotists and wheelchair maintenance team.

Students accepted: Physical and learning disabilities with associated communication or sensory difficulties. We are also a centre of excellence for the use of voice output communication aids.

Applications/selection: To the Principal or receptionist at the above address who will arrange a visit and assessment.

Links with other establishments

Many students take some of their courses at local mainstream colleges.

Out-of-term-contact: There is always someone in the office and the out-of-hours answer-phone is checked daily.

We offer respite care for students during holidays.

The National Society for Epilepsy

Chesham Lane, Chalfont St Peter, Buckinghamshire SL9 0RJ
Tel: 01494 601300 Fax: 01494 871927
Helpline: 01494 601400
Website: www.erg.ion.ucl.ac.uk/nsehome
Chief Executive: Mr. Douglas Bennett
Catchment area: Nationwide   Age range: 17+
Controlled by: National Society for Epilepsy Board of Governors
Fees: NHS-funded Assessment Service

The NSE has four key aims: the eradication of epilepsy in all its forms and, in the meantime, to strive for improvements in the medical treatments; to improve the clinical and care services provided to people with epilepsy by NSE and health professionals elsewhere; to increase public understanding about epilepsy as a medical condition and how to respond appropriately to a seizure; to get accurate, understandable and relevant health information to all people with epilepsy and their carers as and when they need it.

General description

The centre has approximately 270 long term residents, in addition to NHS assessment unit patients. It offers a full range of facilities for people with epilepsy as both inpatients and outpatients.

Staffing: The centre is committed to a multi-disciplinary approach to the needs of people with epilepsy. There are over 350 staff comprising medical and paramedical, administrative and ancillary, nursing and care, social work, teaching and occupational personnel.

Students accepted: There are 33 beds in the assessment unit. Male and female, all of whom have epilepsy. People with additional mental or physical disabilities are also accepted. Longer term care and respite care are also provided.

Applications/selection: People are generally referred by their GPs or hospital consultants. Waiting time varies.

Courses and facilities

The Training Department runs regular courses on all aspects of epilepsy for staff and external organisations. For further information contact the Training Department. The Information and Education Department runs monthly half day seminars covering basic information about epilepsy. For information contact the Information and Education Department.

Links with other establishments

Work placements are found for residents with local employers. College courses, ranging from reading and writing through to GCSE and A levels, are arranged at a local college for residents who wish to take a course.

Out-of-term-contact: The Chalfont Centre does not close for holidays.

Information about the work of the centre can be obtained from the education department.

National Star Centre College of Further Education

Ullenwood Manor, Cheltenham, Gloucestershire GL53 9QU
Tel: 01242 527631 Fax: 01242 222234
Website: www.natstar.ac.uk Email: principal@natstar.ac.uk
Principal: Dr Michael Smith
Catchment area: Nationwide   Age range: 16 +
Controlled by: Independent; DfEE recognition

The emphasis of the College is on the identification of the abilities which individual students need to acquire if they are to achieve their post-college ambitions. Our approach is to relate realistic assessment of the student to the creation of an individually tailored course plan which can call on the whole resources of the College where required.

General description

A specialised residential and day college of further education with adapted and purpose-built facilities on a 30-acre site in the Cotswolds, near Cheltenham. Gymnasium, sauna, swimming pool, art studio, theatre, projectile alley. Accommodation allows students to progress through a series of experiences linked to their individual development. Close links with educational, cultural and leisure facilities in Cheltenham and Gloucester. Videos available on request.

Staffing: Full-time, part-time lecturers; remedial gymnast; swimming instructors; speech therapist; special care managers; nursing officer; medical officer; counsellor/psychologist; admin staff; care staff and professional specialist support.

Students accepted: Physically disabled. Total 125 mixed sex. Ability range - from remedial/pre-vocational to Advanced GNVQ. Specialist centre for students with acquired brain injuries.

Applications/selection: Forms from Principal's Secretary. Invitation for assessment and to meet College staff.

Courses and facilities

Students normally stay for two or three years, each of 36 weeks with one week half-term breaks. Intakes are normally in September, but can be accommodated in January or April.

Care and medical support is complemented by physiotherapy and speech therapy, a counsellor/psychologist, a resource centre specialising in communication aids and the design of individualised solutions to technical problems. There is further learning support available from learning support assistants, occupational therapist and computer and wheelchair technicians.

Course profile: Students build a personal programme developing key skills through key subjects and option units taken from the whole range of College provision, in a manner suited to each individual's pace of learning. Courses meet the requirements of a wide variety of students, whether these be for rehabilitation, addressing major learning difficulties or accessing vocational courses. Access to a range of vocational courses can be gained from the Lifestyles Course or by direct entry. Work experience and external links form part of our 24-hour curriculum experience.

- BTEC Entry Awards, RSA, City and Guilds, NVQs, Pitman, and GCSEs in related subjects. Students can also follow the C&G Wordpower and Numberpower and the RSA National Skills profile
- Foundation, Intermediate, Advanced **GNVQs**, in business, art and design, performing arts, health and social care
- **BTEC** First Diploma and National Diploma in performing arts
- **NVQ**s in sports and recreation levels 1 and 2
- **NVQ**s in information technology level 1-3.

Links with other establishments

Students attend courses at Gloucestershire College of Arts and Technology and Stroud College.

The Nexus Direct Programme

Orlestone Lodge, Hamstreet Road, Orlestone, Nr Ashford, Kent TN26 2EB

Tel: 01233 733477

General Manager: Mr A Rogers Tel: 01233 733908

Catchment area: Nationwide   Age range: 16 +

Controlled by: Private organisation governed by national legislation and monitored by regional social services

Fees: £84,000 pa 52 week care package, social and holiday funding is also inclusive

Aims to provide care and support to young adults with learning difficulties who present mild to severe challenging behaviour. Holistic programme with emphasis on employment, training and competence, leading to independent living.

General description

17th century country house set in 28 acres of grounds. Close to the towns of Ashford and Maidstone as well as the ports and coastal resorts of Folkestone, Dover and Hastings. All single rooms. Spacious accommodation, TV/video lounges, sports and leisure facilities. Participative programme designed to equip residents with a wide range of skills geared towards facilitating their successful integration into community-based services. Three main areas of emphasis: vocational training - college attendance, work-experience, employment acquisition, training, etc; life and social skills training - image enhancement, domestic skills training, community access skills, etc; life planning - fulfilment of ambition, personal development programmes, social support programmes, the "challenge, excitement, fun!" module. Working through links with local horticultural and agricultural college and outdoor pursuits organisation. Holidays included in fees. Programme runs 52 weeks per year.

Staffing: Ratio of 1:2; four academic staff; team leaders; student supporters/carers; sleep-in/waking carers; two maintenance staff.

Residents accepted: Young adults with mild to severe learning difficulties and who present support difficulties by nature of emotional and/or behavioural disorders (criteria for assessment: behaviour environmentally-driven [reactive] as opposed to psychiatric). 27 residents - ability to benefit from the programme.

Applications/selection: By letter/telephone call to the General Manager in the first instance.

Northern Counties School for the Deaf

Great North Road, Newcastle upon Tyne NE2 3BB
Tel: 0191 281 5821 (voice and Minicom) Fax: 0191 281 5060
Principal: Mr. K J C Lewis
Age range: 3-19
Controlled by: The school is a non-maintained residential special school controlled by a governing body
Fees: Prices per term: Day additionally-disabled students - £7520; Day multi-disabled student £8980; Residential additionally-disabled students, Mon-Fri £10,350; Residential multi-disabled students, Mon-Fri fees according to need.

Aims to provide primary, secondary and further education and vocational training for hearing impaired students with other disabilities, who also need to develop independent living skills within a setting using a total communication approach (sign and finger-spelling are used to support oral/aural communication).

General description

A small section of the school is a Special Needs Department which includes facilities and provision for post-16 students. There are five days per week residential facilities on site and each student's programme contains different components, according to individual need, based in the post-16 base, residence and the community. Access is available to all school facilities and support (e.g. medical centre, recreational provision etc.)

Staffing: Staffing varies according to student intake each year, but a high level of teacher/tutor support is available and access to other professionals (e.g. physiotherapist, speech therapist etc.) arranged according to need.

Students accepted: Up to 12 students aged 16 to 19 with hearing impairment/severe communication difficulties and one or more additional disabilities (e.g. visual impairment, learning difficulties, physical disabilities etc.) may be accepted if their educational, training and social needs can be met through the programmes offered.

Applications/selection: Applications are by letter in the first instance addressed to the Principal.

Courses and facilities

Courses are usually vocationally-based, concentrating on the development of work, sheltered work-related skills and independent living. Training takes place within specialist facilities, resdential provision and the local community.

Links with other establishments

There are links with local colleges and training establishments which cater for young people with hearing impairment and/or other disabilities. There are links with the local deaf centre and other groups.

COPE

Nugent House School

Carr Mill Road, Billinge, Wigan WN5 7TT
Tel: 01744 892551 Fax: 01744 895697
Email: head@nugent.wigan.ach.uk
Principal: Mrs J L Bienias
Catchment area: Nationwide   Age range: 7-19
Controlled by: The Nugent Care Society, Liverpool
Fees: Residential -£8396 per term. Day - £6297 per term

COPE

The education of children with emotional and behavioural disorders - including some with a history of mental health difficulties.

General description

Nugent House is a residential and day special school situated in pleasant countryside midway between Liverpool and Manchester. Close proximity to major rail and motorway networks and also International Airport at Manchester. Post-16 students reside in small communities in specialist semi-independent houses. The school is extremely well provided for in terms of facilities, and in addition post-16 students have access to local FE colleges to further their studies. Both termly and 52-week residential care is provided for according to individual needs.

Staffing: 18.5 teaching staff; 47 residential social work staff; 20 classroom support staff; domestic, maintenance, secretarial and financial staff.

Students accepted: Boys with emotional and behavioural disorders, some with specific learning and mental health problems.

Applications/selection: In the first instance by telephone contact with the Headteacher.

Courses and facilities

Nine subjects taken to GCSE level; NVQ; Certificate of Achievement; post-16 students access courses at local colleges. Individual study programmes for those requiring modified curriculum.

Links with other establishments

All local sixth form and FE colleges, psychiatric adolescent unit at Prestwich Hospital, Manchester, other special schools in the region.

Oaklands Park Village Community

Newnham, Gloucestershire GL14 1EF
Tel: 01594 516551 Fax: 01594 516821
Website: www.camphill.org.uk
Catchment area: Unrestricted   Age range: 21 +
Controlled by: Camphill Village Trust

Caring about the environment, work, economic and social life and further education, in communities with adults, some of whom have special needs - real, meaningful work; a shared family life; a rich cultural context.

General description

Oaklands Park is a 130 acre estate set between the Forest of Dean and the River Severn. It is particularly active in farm, market garden, forestry and orchard work, and there is also a woodwork shop and weavery. Between five and twelve residents live in family houses with co-workers and their children. Christian festivals are celebrated, and there is a very wide range of evening activities: study groups, lectures, dancing, games, music, acting, sports, reading etc.

Students accepted: 53 men and women with learning disabilities.

Applications/selection: Applications to The Admissions Group, Oaklands Park, Newnham, Glos GL14 1EF can be made at the age of 18 onwards. Being put on the waiting list is not joining a queue. The particular needs of each applicant awaiting admission are considered. Forms are completed prior to interview by the medical adviser. The waiting list is only made up of those who have had a successful trial visit to a village centre - visits are arranged as soon as possible after interview, usually for a fortnight initially, then for a three-month period when accommodation is available.

Courses and facilities

No courses as such are provided, the Village being a community within which each resident can be assisted to individual independence and social adjustment.

Links with other establishments

Considerable contact with other 11 CVT centres.

Out-of-term contact: Not necessary. Information is always available from the Village. The Village does not close at any time of the year.

Oakwood Court

7/9 Oak Park Villas, Dawlish, Devon EX7 0DE
Tel: 01626 864066 Fax: 01626 866770
Principal: Mr J F Loft BEd
Educational Psychologist: Mr D M Hughes BA
Catchment area: Nationwide   Age range: 16-25 +

Aims to provide a safe, empowering environment in which young people with learning disabilities and associated behavioural, emotional and/or social difficulties, can confidently complete the transition from adolescence into the adult world.

General description

A co-educational, residential specialist educational and care provision for up to 30 young people. The college has a number of sites in the South Devon area: each site fulfils a particular role in students' programmes of study. Opportunities for developing sporting and leisure interests exist in the locality, and students are encouraged and enabled to make good use of these. There are excellent rail and road links to the major centres in the region and to all parts of Britain. Students have their own study bedrooms, some with en-suite bathrooms. The residential accommodation is designed to facilitate the development of independent living skills.

Keyworker and Personal Tutor systems ensure an individualised approach to care and education and promote student advocacy. Advocacy skills are further developed through the student council. A generous staff to student ratio allows high levels of physical care and individual attention. Counselling and other community based specialist services are used whenever a need is identified. Review conferences are held annually.

Students accepted: Young people who require specialist further education. Continuous care and training provided beyond 25 years.

Applications/selection: Prospective students are invited to visit Oakwood for a short assessment period (3 to 5 days). Referrals are usually initiated by Specialist Careers Officers, Local Education Authorities or Social Services. A student's first term is used as an extended assessment period. Students attend on either 38 week (term time) or 52 week (extended placement) basis.

Courses and facilities

(Details of all courses forwarded on request)

The educational framework recognises that each student's style and rate of learning, consequent progress and achievement, may vary. Each student follows an individualised programme of learning.

Core skills: The development and improvement of these skills form an integral part of all areas of study. Information technology equipment is available and is used to enhance learning. Students are able to gain recognised accreditation in numeracy, literacy and IT.

Vocational courses: The college offers a range of courses leading to the Vocational Foundation Certificate award. Students may progress to NVQ courses. In addition, the college collaborates with the local sector college and other training providers to extend the range of qualifications available. Work experience incorporated into courses.

Independency and social skills: Students undertake programmes to prepare them for either supported living, semi-independence or fully independent living. Flexible use of the college's residential facilities ensures that students can progress through independency training at a pace suited to their individual needs. Students receive formal timetabled social skills lessons to explore and develop insights into all aspects of personal and social relationships. Social skills training permeates all areas of college life; students are encouraged to value their own wishes and options whilst acknowledging the needs and rights of others.

A broad educational experience: Optional courses, based on recreation, sport, creativity and self-expression are included in students timetables.

Further Information: A prospectus is available on request. Informal visits by prior arrangement; please contact the college secretary.

The Orpheus Centre

North Park Lane, Godstone Surrey RH9 8ND
Tel: 01883 744664 Fax: 01883 744994
Website: www.orpheus.org.uk
E-mail: staff@orpheus.org.uk
Centre Director: Mrs Megan Johnson
Age range: Apprentices 18-25 Course students 18-40
Catchment area: United Kingdom & Europe
Controlled by: The Orpheus Trust
Fees: Available on request

General description

This is a residential performing arts centre in Godstone, Surrey designed for disabled and non-disabled young people of the age ranges specified above. We offer full-time apprenticeships for up to three years and a wide choice of courses.

This is a fully accessible residential performing arts centre – the first of its kind. The Georgian farmhouse has very comfortable accommodation. The gardens have sculptures, marvellous views and an open-air swimming pool. There is a bar and the food is delicious. It's the perfect place in which to make friends and to be creative.

Staffing: The Centre Director has a strong team of carers, managers and other staff.

Students accepted: The Centre welcomes applications from students who have physical impairments and are within the age range. For non-disabled students studying music, drama or other subjects we offer the experience of providing personal support for our disabled students. And you share with them the enjoyment of creating new pieces of work.

Application/selection: For the courses there is a simple form to complete. To become an apprentice involves applying for the details, making an application to the Centre Director and participating in a four week assessment period. We also recommend that applicants try and attend one of our courses prior to the assessment.

Courses and facilities

Courses include music theatre, drama, songwriting, dance, keyboards and light & sound. Each course consists of approximately sixteen young disabled people, sixteen student enablers, three tutors and the centre staff. The tutors are all experienced working professionals, and under their guidance the participants create songs, stories and dances, which are then performed in front of an audience. There is a theatre, rehearsal space and a recording studio.

Links with other establishments

We have many strong links with other charities and the local community, schools and colleges.

Overley Hall School

Wellington, Telford, Shropshire TF6 5HE
Tel and Fax: 01952 740 262
Head: Mr. W O'Hagan BA(Hons)
Age range: 9-19
Catchment area: No restrictions given. All UK and overseas
Controlled by: Included on list of approved independent schools issued by the DfEE
Fees: On application

General description

Overley Hall is a classic Victorian mansion, set in 16 acres of garden and woodland; we cater for those with PMLD, challenging behaviour and/or autism. Overley Hall is multi-denominational. There is a Snoezelen room and hydrotherapy pool; three minibuses; home and other transport arranged if required.

A successful OFSTED was conducted in September 1996 and September 1999. Professor Emeritus Joan D Bicknall is an honorary adviser.

A complete prospectus, with fee structure, is available from the Head.

Staffing: 1:3 to 1:1 ratio as required. Speech and other therapy.

Students accepted: Children with severe and profound multiple learning difficulties, also with challenging behaviour and autism.

Application/selection: Contact the Head for further information. Full prospectus available on request.

Courses and facilities

National and/or developmental and lifeskills curriculum.

Ovingdean Hall School

Greenways, Brighton, East Sussex BN2 7BJ
Tel: 01273 301929 Fax: 01273 305884
Headteacher: Malcolm Bown BA
Age range: 16+
Catchment area: As appropriate to a weekly residential establishment
Controlled by: Governing body; non-maintained
Fees: £4,815 per term for day pupils; £6,321 per term for weekly boarders; £7,962 per term for full boarders (who are fostered with local families at weekends and during half term holidays)

Aims to further the student's education and social awareness, using on-site and off-site facilities according to the needs of the individual student.

General description

The further education section of the school provides the opportunities for students to extend their academic qualifications, to broaden their vocational experiences and to develop their social confidence. The students have their own teaching areas and residential accommodation thus encouraging self-reliance and independence.

Staffing: All FE tutors are qualified teachers of the deaf and experienced in post-16 education. Other teachers of the deaf are drawn from the main school staff. The FE section also uses the school's audiology staff, medical staff, educational psychologist and speech therapist. Out-of-school support is given by a team again experienced with post-16 students.

Students accepted: Hearing-impaired students, some of whom may have additional minimal special needs, but require a natural oral method of teaching (sign language is not employed). All academic abilities. Up to 20 students, both sexes.

Applications/selection: Applications are made to the Headteacher. Early application is advised to allow for assessment/discussion for the appropriate course and for the administration procedure to be completed before the end of the Summer term. Existing school pupils are given priority for placement.

Courses and facilities

Students can follow one of a range of courses relevant to their needs and chosen career path. This can involve extended (as opposed to repeated) GCSE, mature syllabus GCSE, GNVQs or City & Guilds Skillpower. The school offers GNVQ courses at Foundation and Intermediate level in the following areas - business studies, manufacturing, performing arts, health and social care, science, art and design and information technology. Full-time students at Brighton College of Technology are supported by specialist teachers of the deaf from Ovingdean.

Courses are individually tailored for each subject and all offer teacher of the deaf support at an appropriate level. Most courses involve an extensive work experience programme and all students also spend one day a week at a local college. All FE students live in a separate residence in Central Brighton, which can accommodate 30 students in single study bedrooms.

Links with other establishments

Brighton College of Technology. As above and the school will also provide support to hearing-impaired students following mainstream courses at the above colleges.

Out-of-term contact: Most special needs careers offices in the South East are aware of provisions available. For current FE prospectus contact the school secretary.

The Papworth Trust

Papworth Everard, Cambridge CB3 8RG
Tel: 01480 830341 Fax: 01480 830781
Director of Progression and Employment: Stephen Dunn
Age range: 18 +

Papworth is one of the leading disability charities in the Eastern Region helping people to achieve independence and fulfil ambitions by enabling them to access appropriate training, employment and housing.

Courses and facilities

Papworth offers residential progression programmes for young people with disabilities leaving school or college, to help them develop their skills in a wide range of activities. Residents operate their own Advocacy Service. 24-hour residential care is available for those with substantial care needs.

Independent living skills are developed through courses in cookery, money and household maintenance. Training flats offer the chance to practise these skills until people are ready to move into their own home. As a specialist housing association for people with disabilities, Papworth enables people to live independently in the community, locally and throughout the region.

For people who are not yet ready for work Papworth offers daytime progression programmes, comprising one to one personal development, education and specific vocational training, leading to NVQs in administration, IT, retailing, distributive operations, customer service and Key Skills. Through an initial assessment with an occupational psychologist, people can identify their abilities and aptitudes and use the information to make informed choices about their programme and future goals. Papworth provides training and job coaching to support people in making the move to open employment, supported employment or volunteering. All programmes can be residential or non-residential.

Freestanding of other programmes, Papworth also offers vocational assessment to people with disabilities, whether from birth or acquired, to help them make more informed choices about their future.

Pengwern Further Education College

Rhuddlan, Nr Rhyl, Denbighshire LL18 5UH
Tel: 01745 590281 Fax: 01745 591736
Principal: Melvyn Booker
Catchment area: No restrictions   Age range: 16-25
Controlled by: MENCAP
Fees: £22,911 per annum (invoiced quarterly); student's DSS benefits may be used to offset part of the fee, with FEFC being the main provider of funding who may seek joint funding from the local authority concerned. Individual fees negotiated for students with additional special needs. Pengwern College is an Investor in People.

To provide an educational curriculum for transition to adulthood for adolescents with learning disabilities (including severe and profound) in a variety of residential and daytime facilities. The curriculum includes pre-vocational and vocational education as appropriate with a strong emphasis on personal development. Functional communication skills, physiotherapy, speech therapy and other services are provided.

General description

Pengwern College is a residential further education college, offering an alternative structured FE course for students with learning disabilities. It was awarded a grade 2 by the FEFC in July 1999. Situated five miles south of Rhyl (nearest railway station), close to the A55, within 30 minutes of Chester. The campus contains the first residential stages of student's development: the Coach Houses, Education Block and Garden Farm. Assessed development by the student leads to residential stages of increasing contact with the community (e.g. work experience; social interaction) in small houses in neighbouring communities, Rhuddlan, St. Asaph, Prestatyn. Facilities include Turner's Café (in St. Asaph) staffed and run by students and a bed and breakfast facility (in St. Asaph). Students continue to access the educational block and farm park throughout their course. Total of 20 different/varied living and training situations. One house with facilities for students using wheelchairs; all facilities suitable for wheelchairs.

Staffing: Total of 54 staff including daytime tutors. Medical, dental services etc. provided locally. Specialist skill input, e.g. communications skills, physiotherapy etc. when required.

Students accepted: Total capacity 46; both sexes. Learning disability as the primary disability, and additionally, behavioural, physical and complex disabilities depending upon each individual's situation and need.

Applications/selection: Initial visit by the proposed student with parents and/or social workers. A three-day assessment period is arranged, followed by a review and a decision made regarding the offer of a place. The initial three-month period is used for further assessment and educational programming according to student's needs. Detailed assessment throughout the period of education, and partnership with the sponsoring body, local authority and parents, in the interests of the student, is emphasised.

Courses and facilities

As students develop the appropriate personal, social and daily living skills, they progress through the residential and vocational units within the college.

Residential training continues for 42 weeks (38 from Sept 2000) of the year, seven days a week. The length of the course is up to three years dependent upon the individual assessment of each student.

All students work through an individual programme based on the principles of inclusive learning. Students access NVQ qualifications as appropriate in the areas of catering and hospitality, agriculture, horticulture, leisure and tourism and office administration.

There are regular reviews of progress and, for the purposes of forward planning and setting objectives, students can also access work experience in community situations.

Links with other establishments

Employment Services; MENCAP local services, where appropriate; community adult literacy; agencies in student's home community.

Pennine Camphill Community

Boyne Hill, Chapelthorpe, Wakefield WF4 3JH
Tel: 01924 255281 Fax: 01924 240257
Website: www.pennine.org.uk
Email: office@pennine.org.uk
Catchment area: Nationwide
Controlled by: Pennine Camphill Community Ltd. Registered Charity Member of Association of Camphill Communities
Fees: As FEFC matrix or by negotiation

Aims to create a lively, interesting, educationally relevant and structured environment of young people who come as students; to encourage personal development and maturation and provide core skills for the many different situations that students leave to.

General description

Pennine Camphill Community is situated on the outskirts of Wakefield in the 35 acre estate of Boyne Hill House. It is served by a regular bus service and borders Newmillerdam Country Park.

Staffing: 24 full-time co-workers with additional part-time voluntary workers.

Students accepted: There are 42 residential students with additional day places available. Adolescents with emotional, behavioural, mental health and maturation difficulties, as well as students with learning difficulties.

Applications/selection: To the Secretary including a social history, recent school report and relevant medical history. Visits are welcomed and can be arranged through the office.

Courses and facilities

Up to five years broad-based integrated pre-vocational course is offered (prospectus available on request). Provision is made to allow the more mature student to complete the course in a shorter time. Facilities include classrooms, hall, movement hall, craft workshops, agricultural and horticultural holding, and riding stables. Extended curriculum includes evening activities.

Links with other establishments

Some students in their final year attend part-time courses at Wakefield District College and/or gain work experience in the locality. An active involvement is taken in further placements where possible.

Out-of-term-contact: As term time.

Peredur Garden and Craft Centre (Part of the Peredur Trust)

Trebullom, Altarnun, Launceston, Cornwall PL15 7RF
Tel: 01566 86575 Fax: 01566 86975
Managers: Joan & Siegfried Rudel
Catchment area: Nationwide   Age range: 19+
Controlled by: Independent
Registered with Cornwall Social Services
Fees: £336 per week

Aims to provide a facility for young adults, who are unable to meet the stresses of living and working in the ordinary community, to have a full and satisfying life and the opportunity of gradual social integration into the surrounding community.

General description

A centre run on the principles of Rudolf Steiner. Trebullom is a small estate of 11 acres. Once the centre of a large farm, the main house has been altered and extended to provide accommodation for the students. The farm buildings are being adapted for animal husbandry and processing of farm produce. There is a 2-acre market garden with glasshouses, and fruit orchards/soft fruit. A reference library is available for the use of students. The small market town of Launceston is easily accessible, with Exeter, Plymouth and the coast not far away. Opportunities for cycling, walking and swimming. There is encouragement to make contacts with local people.

Staffing: includes the two managers, a visiting doctor and residential care staff.

Students accepted: Male students only.

Applications/selection: Write to the Manager enclosing a case history and relevant reports.

Courses and facilities

No formal courses, comprehensive activities in horticulture and crafts, with further education. It is hoped that students will be helped towards a future return to ordinary life and work.

Therapeutic practical training covers the growing of a wide range of vegetables and greenhouse crops, plant propagation, soft and orchard fruit. Horses, sheep, poultry and bees are also kept. A good part of the working day is spent in practical and social activities (such as music and singing) and training.

Links with other establishments

With other nearby establishments of the Peredur Trust and the local community. Member of Committee for Steiner Special Education, and of BFCHP.

Out-of-term-contact: Information during holiday periods can be obtained from the secretary at the above address.

All residents return home for holidays on a regular basis.

Peredur Farm and Craft Centre (Part of Peredur Trust)

Basill Manor, St Clether, Launceston, Cornwall PL15 8QJ
(Office at Trebullom, Altarnun, Launceston, Cornwall PL15 7RF)
Tel: 01566 86575 Fax: 01566 86975
Managers: Joan & Siegfried Rudel
Catchment area: Nationwide   Age range: 19+
Controlled by: Independent
Registered with Cornwall Social Services
Fees: £336 per week

Aims to provide a facility for young adults, who are unable to meet the stresses of living and working in the ordinary community, to have a full and satisfying life and the opportunity of gradual social integration into the surrounding community.

General description

An establishment operating on the principles of Rudolf Steiner, which aims to help emotionally-disturbed young adults to have a full and satisfying life. Residents take an active part in the running of the household, cooking, baking and laundry work. The Manor House has been restored and modernised to provide a beautiful home. Outbuildings are used as pottery, weaving and wood workshops (making a variety of useful objects and small toys), and the 8 acres of land are used to produce vegetables, milk, honey, eggs, and wool for the weaving workshop. The Manor has its own social life of musical and other leisure activities.

The Trust also runs a mixed farm of 164 acres which is registered as an organic farm with the Soil Association. All feedstuffs are grown on the farm. Residents take part in all farm activities although the running of the farm does not depend on them.

Students accepted: Emotionally-disturbed young adults. Male only. No upper age limit.

Applications/selection: Write to the Manager enclosing a case history and relevant reports.

Courses and facilities

No courses as such. This centre provides social adaptation through the experience of living and working in a community. New skills would however be learned as part of workshop, farm and domestic training. Some residents may progress far enough to take up local employment. The main intention is not to provide long term placements, although this can be arranged when required.

Links with other establishments

Contacts with the local community. Member of Committee for Steiner Special Education, and of BFCHP.

All residents return home for holidays on a regular basis.

Philip Green Memorial School

Boveridge House, Cranborne, Wimborne, Dorset BH21 5RU
Tel: 01725 517218 Fax: 01725 517968
Principal: Mrs L Walter
Catchment area: Unrestricted   Age range: 11-19
Controlled by: Boveridge House School Trust
Fees: £6100 per term full boarding

Aims to provide a supportive learning environment where individual students can develop academic and social skills for life.

General description

The school is sited in a listed house set in 35 acres of beautiful Dorset countryside. The main house is used for residential accommodation with the classrooms being situated in outbuildings within the grounds. The school is close to and has many links with the village of Cranborne and the local community.

Staffing: 24 staff.

Students accepted: Students with moderate/severe learning difficulties and speech and language problems. Maximum of 40 mixed students.

Applications/selection: By interview. Parents of prospective students are invited to visit the school during term time, but are requested to make an appointment by telephone beforehand.

Courses and facilities

Students follow National Curriculum courses to Key Stage IV. Differentiated to meet their individual needs. Courses offer the opportunity for students to take Certificate of Educational Achievement, GCSE and ASDAN qualifications as appropriate.

Post-16 provision offers Key Skills Learning in English and mathematics with additional learning in the areas of careers, employment, vocational skills and life skills.

Assessment is completed in academic and life skills twice annually. Specific learning targets are then set for each student in these areas for each term. Parents/guardians are kept informed of these aims and progress. The school works closely with local schools and colleges to provide a wide learning base for pupils which matches their individual need. Students attend other educational settings on a regular basis to develop their skills in the wider community setting.

Social activities are carried out within school and the local community to provide a supported extended curriculum for social skills learning.

Links with other establishments

Pupils attend local colleges of further education.

Philpots Manor Schools and FE Training Course

West Hoathly, Nr. East Grinstead, West Sussex RH19 4PR
Tel: 01342 810268 Office: 01342 811382
Fax: 01342 811363
Administrator: Mr S Blaxland de Lange
Age range: 16-19
Catchment area: A radius of approximately 60 miles around the school
Controlled by: Independent School
Fees: Variable, but not less than £11,000 per term

Aims to help young people for whom the development of human qualities is judged to be more important than involvement in the stress of today's educational system, with the prospect of re-integrating them into the mainstream whenever possible.

General description

Situated in rural Sussex, the school is set in 30 acres of gardens, orchards, a farm and surrounding woodlands. An old manor house provides the main residence, close by are four modern bungalows where the children live in family groups. The training course (16-19 years) has a large self-contained building set a little aside from the manor house. The school is accommodated in spacious classrooms and has associated technical, craft and recreation facilities.

Staffing: Approximately 66, half teaching and half residential.

Students accepted: Children and young people with special needs, who are emotionally disturbed/deprived, those with nervous or anxiety symptoms, habit or organic disorders. Borderline autism, controlled epilepsy, but not with physical disabilities or with behavioural problems, and are working six to 24 months below average.

Applications/selection: Applications by LEA of SSD with the usual reports of psychologist, psychiatrist, etc. Interviews and admission if found suitable, providing the school has vacancies.

Courses and facilities

The school follows the Waldorf Curriculum. City and Guilds courses available for suitable candidates.

Links with other establishments

The school is a member of the Committee for Steiner Special Education. Children, if able, can continue at local FE colleges whilst boarding at the school. The teaching and residential staff take part in courses throughout the year.

Out-of-term contact: Whilst school terms are run on the usual 3 terms a year, there is always someone at the school during holidays to give information.

Pield Heath House RC School

Victor Braun Centre, Extended Education Department, Pield Heath Road, Uxbridge, Middlesex UB8 3NW
Tel: 01895 258507   Fax: 01895 256497
Email: pieldheath@btconnect.com
Principal: Sister Julie Rose
Age range: 16-19 +
Catchment area: National and international
Controlled by: Congregation of the Sacred Hearts of Jesus and Mary. DfEE recognition
Fees: On request

Aims to promote the spiritual, moral, cultural, mental and physical development. To empower all students to be active participants within their community and prepare the individual for the opportunities, choices, responsibilities and experience of adult life.

General description

The Victor Braun Centre forms part of the main school. Accommodation is in small family-grouped homes, single or double rooms, facilities within each house provide social learning skills for day and residential students. Full programme of after school activities for residential pupils.

Staffing: Teaching staff; ancillary workers; speech therapist; nursing staff.

Students accepted: Mixed. Residential - weekly. M/SLD -language disordered pupils - communication skills - speciality.

Application/selection: Visit to school and informal interview.

Courses and facilities

As a centre responding to change, we have a brand new purpose built centre. There is a reception area, team enterprise centre, hair salon, careers office, science room, art room with built in kiln, as well as an ICT and state of the art food technology centre and kitchen. The excellent facilities available allow students to be trained on site and have the opportunity to gain practical experience in a wide range of vocational courses. Use is made of nationally-recognised qualifications to underpin and validate the work of the centre. Currently the range of these qualifications is: The National Skills Profile, The ASDAN Towards Independence Scheme, AEB Tests in Numeracy and Literacy, GCSE PE, PE Certificate of Achievement, GCSE Art, Art Certificate of Achievement, Pitman Text Production Skills, National Record of Achievement. It is tutorial based and there is pastoral care to help students develop positive self image and aid transition. Students follow individual programmes based on negotiated and revised action plans. Constant revision and updating of curriculum, delivery and resources to meet the challenges of special education for the future.

Links with other establishments

We have strong links with local schools and colleges. We constantly update our resource base of contacts with professionals in students' home areas. We are an active member of the local special education Compact. We have developed links with other schools offering Team Enterprise. We have our own Business Advisor who visits regularly and keeps us informed of various Team Enterprise events. We have recently received the 'Investors in People' Award and we are always keen to foster greater links with the local community.

Portland College

Nottingham Road, Mansfield, Nottinghamshire NG18 4TJ
Tel: 01623 499111 Fax: 01623 499133
Website: www.portland.org.uk
Email: college@portland.org.uk
Director: Mr. M E A Syms
Age range: 16-59
Catchment area: UK and international where appropriate
Controlled by: An independent college
Fees: Further Education/Foundation Education Unit -six categories of fees from £16,000 to £50,950. Applications for FE assessment should be sent to the college for the attention of the Admissions Officer

Aims to maximise ability and minimise disability in a residential setting for individual empowerment through employment, education and training, independence and integration.

General description

Three miles south of Mansfield on the A60 in a woodland setting. Purpose built and single storey buildings accessible to students with mobility problems. Special facilities include wide doors, covered walkways, special baths/showers, equipment to maximise independence. Leisure centre, recreation hall, outdoor sports including bowling, football, wheelchair games. Youth club through which there are strong links with local community. Specialised transport for off-campus activities.

Staffing: Approximately 270.

Students accepted: Students with physical disabilities, with exception of totally blind students. At present 230 students from below average to above average IQ.

Applications/selection: Interview and assessment prior to acceptance.

Courses and facilities

Funding for vocational programmes is through the DfEE Work based Learning for Adults programme. Funding for further education is through the FEFC via the LEA.

Vocational courses offered leading to NVQ:

- business administration
- accounts
- information technology
- horticulture
- engineering manufacture
- electronics
- computer aided drafting and design
- further and continuing education
- individual tailored programmes

Where appropriate, courses lead to NVQs. External accreditation is used wherever applicable, eg City and Guilds, RSA, London Chamber of Commerce and Industry. Specialist equipment available, eg Touch Talker, Lightwriter, computers, CCTV.

Links with other establishments

Links with all providers of education for special needs.

115

Queen Alexandra College of Further Education

Court Oak Road, Harborne, Birmingham B17 9TG
Tel: 0121 428 5050   Fax: 0121 428 5047
Information line: 0121 312 1234
Website: www.qac.ac.uk
Email: enquiries@qac.ac.uk
Principal: Mrs S Wright
Catchment area: Nationwide   Age range: 16 +
Fees: on application

Aims to provide assessment, guidance, pre-vocational and vocational programmes.

General description

Three miles from the city in a quiet residential area. Accommodation ranges from high support on campus hostels to independent houses in the community. QAC offers a wide range of social activities within a 24 hour curriculum.

Staffing: In excess of 100 care and teaching staff including counsellor, qualified nurses, BSL, mobility trainers.

Students accepted: Subject to assessment, 120 students aged from 16-63 from all areas. Visual impairment, deafblindness, Aspergers, autism, dyslexia plus additional disabilities and/or learning difficulties.

Applications/selection: Via admissions office. Individual assessments last a minimum of two days for FEFC funded students.

Courses and facilities

Pre-vocational

* Pre-GNVQ entry level programmes

* GNVQ - Foundation, Intermediate, Advanced: Art and Design, Business Studies, Information Technology, Health and Social Care, Performing Arts, Leisure and Tourism.

Vocational (NVQs and Certificates)

Manufacturing programmes: Engineering Technologies, Computer Aided Design, Computer Numerical Control, Assembly and Manufacturing Skills, Signmaking, Glass Decoration, wood Craft and Design, Cycle Mechanics, Horticulture.

Service sector programmes: Administration, Information Technology, telesales, Retailing

Links with other establishments

Supported programmes in any of 19 local colleges of further education make an enormous range of programmes available.

Out-of-term-contact: College is open all year round.

Assessment and work preparation programmes: Referrals invited nationally.

Queen Elizabeth's Training College

Leatherhead Court, Leatherhead, Surrey KT22 0BN
Tel: 01372 841100 Fax: 01372 844156
Principal: Mr R D Beckinsale
Catchment area: Unrestricted   Age range: 18 +
Controlled by: Queen Elizabeth's Foundation for Disabled People
Fees: For private/overseas students around £480 per week (residential) or around £320 per week (non-residential). Prices vary for different courses and are available on application.

Committed to training for work, the college provides business studies and technical courses for disabled students who are considered capable of enhancing their employment skills. Wherever possible, all courses lead to National Vocational Qualifications.

General description

Near junction 9 of the M25 on the A245 Leatherhead to Cobham road off the A3. Specially designed buildings incorporating the latest technology and equipment in all classrooms and workshops for training. Attractive purpose-built and well-equipped residential accommodation with resident staff always on duty. Sports and social club, gymnasium, sports facilities, video and TV rooms, and an active students' association.

Staffing: Principal; one head of training; one marketing research & development manager; one head of work placement; three work placement advisors; 27 instructors; two open learning tutors; one job club controller; one head of work preparation; one leisure manager; one leisure officer; one office manager; four secretaries; five administrators; two wardens; three SRNs; two cleaning supervisers; cleaners and contract cleaners; contract caterers and one bar steward; one storeman and assistant; one maintenance supervisor and three assistants. A consultant physician and psychiatrist are always available. A GP visits weekly.

Students accepted: All except for the totally blind.

Applications/selection: Application for training should be made through the Disability Employment Adviser at a Jobcentre. Training fees and personal allowances are paid by the Employment Training system of the DfEE's TEED.

Courses and facilities

The College offers the following courses:

Business studies: accountancy level 2 & 3; business administration level 2; business administration/information technology level 1; information technology level 2; marketing, sales and customer service; computer installation, upgrade & mainenance; leisure & business travel.

Technical: horticulture; audio visual techniques; wood occupations; computer aided design; domestic appliance servicing (white goods); electronics; vehicle refinishing; welding.

Links with other establishments

The college is a unit of Queen Elizabeth's Foundation for Disabled People, Leatherhead, Surrey.

Application helpline - College Administration 01372 841100.

RNIB Alwyn House

3 Wemysshall Road, Ceres, by Cupar, Fife KY15 5LX
Tel: 0133 482 8894   Fax: 0133 482 8911
Centre Manager: Craig Stockton
Catchment area: The Centre accepts clients from Scotland and the North of England   Age range: 16+
Controlled by: Royal National Institute for the Blind

Fees: Normally paid by the DfEE. Clients are usually paid a weekly allowance if they opt to discontinue certain state benefits for the duration of their course. In the case of Training for Work clients, the fees are paid by the Training Enterprise Councils (TECs) in England and the Local Enterprise Companies (LECs) in Scotland. Local education bursaries and SEO grants are available for further education students

Aims to provide training, further education and rehabilitation for blind and partially-sighted persons. The courses aim to determine occupational aptitudes and vocational preference, identify existing skills and ability to acquire new skills, give guidance on possible areas of employment, and go on to provide training for work programmes and further education courses where required.

General description

Alwyn House is situated in the quiet village of Ceres in Fife, three miles from Cupar and seven miles from St Andrews. Cupar railway station is on the main line from London to Aberdeen and has good rail links with most centres of population in Scotland and the North of England. Clients arriving at Cupar are normally transported from the station by the centre's minibus. There is an adequate bus service from Ceres to Cupar, Kirkcaldy, St Andrews and Dundee. The centre has accommodation for 16 clients and the residence is centrally heated throughout. All bedrooms have washhand basins. There are comfortable lounges with facilities for watching TV, listening to audio entertainment and a games room with pool, darts and exercise equipment available. There is a spacious garden with a bowling green which clients can enjoy in their free time.

Staffing: The centre has 20 staff and has available, on call, a GP. The centre now has the services of a low-vision adviser who carries out low-vision assessment.

Students accepted: Blind and partially-sighted adults (male and female). Clients with guide dogs can be accommodated.

Applications/selection: Applications to the centre for employment rehabilitation are normally made through Disability Employment Advisers at Jobcentres in conjunction with social welfare officers for blind persons. Clients may make preliminary visits to view the facilities. Clients can make direct application through the centre manager.

Courses and facilities

The course provision is continually adapting and expanding and all programmes are tailored to the individual and his/her needs and desires. At present courses are offered in information technology, basic skills and communication, office skills, horticulture and woodwork, including Computer Aided Drawing (CAD). Additionally clients can benefit from training in mobility, literacy, numeracy, independent living, and job seeking. Clients may opt to include counselling and a work placement in their programme.

The present programmes available are: one week initial assessment and action plan preparation; work preparation, lasting up to 12 weeks; job retention course – for employees who need to gain new skills or retrain to retain existing job; personal development – designed to develop skills that allow the individual to play an active part in their local community.

Links with other establishments

FE colleges - Elmwood College, Cupar; Motherwell College. Local societies for the welfare of the blind, the Guide Dogs for the Blind Association and Sheltered Workshops.

Out-of-term-contact: Craig Stockton, Centre Manager (01334 828894).

RNIB Condover Hall School

Condover, Nr Shrewsbury, Shropshire SY5 7AH.
Tel: 01743 872320 Fax: 01743 873310
Principal: Dr A Best
Catchment area: Nationwide   Age range: 5-24
Controlled by: Royal National Institute for the Blind
Fees: Day attendance from £21,127; weekly boarding from £29,319; full-boarding from £32,577.

To give students the fullest possible opportunities for learning, based on activity and experience; and to encourage them to grow into independent people within the limits of their disabilities.

General description

The school is located in a village about five miles from Shrewsbury. The campus includes teaching, administrative and staff training accommodation, together with family flats, sports hall and swimming pool all set in extensive grounds. The school has a special Low Vision Unit and Information Technology Suite. All accommodation is planned or adapted to meet the student's special needs.

Students are cared for in small family groups, with qualified residential care staff. Close contact between parents and their child is maintained, and parents are encouraged to keep in close touch with staff. Accommodation is available for parents and families to stay at the school. Students are grouped in classes according to age bands and taking into account individual disabilities and educational needs. In the primary and secondary departments, teaching is class-based; for 16-19 year old students in the continuing education department, most lessons are based on subject groups with specialist staff. Many aspects of the curriculum are delivered through practical activities using the extensive school campus and facilities in the community.

Residential accommodation is provided over 52 weeks in both the school and FE centre.

Staffing: RNIB provides a multi-disciplinary team of staff who seek to create a stimulating environment within which every child has their individual needs met. There is a teaching staff of 14 teachers with full-time and part-time classroom assistants. Residential care is provided by staff who have received specialist training. The school has physiotherapists, speech therapists, a mobility officer and a part-time educational psychologist. A member of staff has full-time responsibility for liaison work to assist students preparing to leave the school, and to support their families and local authorities in the search for the most appropriate placement.

Students accepted: The school provides for boys and girls aged 5-19 years who have various degrees of visual disability together with one or more additional impairment. The Pathways Services provides education for deaf-blind students within specialised classes and family units or, where appropriate, through placements with other students in the school. A separate Further Education centre for young people aged 18-24 years is attached to the school.

Applications/selection: A member of staff is available to discuss the school with parents and local authorities. She can arrange visits to the school, visit the family in their home and carry out a preliminary assessment in the child's school.

Courses and facilities

Curriculum: The school curriculum covers all National Curriculum areas (except a foreign language) and concentrates on work at levels 1 and 2. In addition, students are encouraged to develop the use of any sight and hearing they have and may receive instruction in specialist curriculum areas such as mobility. A scheme of self-care and social skills development is delivered primarily by the school's specially trained residential care staff. The FE Unit provides courses based on ASDAN Towards Independence Scheme and Accreditation for Life and Living Skills (ALL).

COPE

119

RNIB Manor House

Skills Development Centre, Manor House, Middle Lincombe Road, Torquay, Devon TQ1 2NG
Tel: 01803 214523 Fax: 01803 214143
Website: www.rnib.org.uk
Email: manorhouse@rnib.org.uk
Centre Manager: Jill Read
Age range: 16+
Controlled by: Royal National Institute for the Blind
Fees: On application

Aims to provide specialised individual assessment, rehabilitation and training services for adults with serious sight problems.

General description

The centre, based in a Victorian manor house overlooking the sea, provides leading edge, comprehensive residential and outreach services for visually impaired people throughout the UK. All programmes are planned with each client's needs and aspirations in mind. Modules available include mobility, visual and tactile skills development, IT, keyboard skills, Braille, independent living, English & maths, woodwork, leathercraft, engineering and horticulutre. All programmes are supported by qualified care staff, counsellors and psychologists.

Staffing: Qualified multi-disciplinary staffing as appropriate to the widely varying needs of clients.

Students accepted: Any adult over 16. The lower age limit does not necessarily apply to non-resident clients. Visually-impaired and those with additional impairments e.g. full wheelchair access, and facilities for people with additional hearing impairment.

Applications/selection: All enquiries welcome from individuals or disability professionals seeking advice on visual impairment services. Most of the centre's clients are referred by Disability Employment advisors, social services departments or representatives of local authority education.

Courses and facilities

Enhanced assessment: Social and/or vocational - up to one week.

Social rehabilitation: Individually tailored programmes, which may include training in mobility, independent living skills, Braille and communication skills. The aim is that clients work towards becoming safe, independent, fully integrated members of society.

Work preparation programmes: Individually-planned programmes, usually of up to nine weeks but flexible according to need(s) of client. Job retention courses to achieve redeployment. Vocational training in wood occupations, plastic injection moulding and leathergoods manufacture for NVQ. The length of each person's course is adjusted to meet the client's situation and according to the required course content. The range of courses, services and facilities is constantly developing and the centre will welcome enquiries about new developments or any other matter at any time.

Links with other establishments

Support for students at South Devon College, Torquay. Steadily growing number of educational, commercial and industrial organisations with whom we work closely to supplement our curriculum and to provide work experience.

120

RNIB New College

Whittington Road, Worcester WR5 2JX

Tel: 01905 763933   Fax: 01905 763277

Principal: Mr Nick Ratcliffe MA

Age range: 11-19

Catchment area: Nationwide and New College welcomes students from abroad

Controlled by: RNIB

Fees: Payable by LEA/FEFC

Our mission is to fit every New College student into the world beyond school by fostering the skills and confidence needed to overcome disabilities and to fulfil potential.

General description

New College is a school for 115 academically-able blind and visually-impaired boys and girls providing access to the full National Curriculum. Students take eight or nine GCSEs and three Advanced level courses from a range of over 20.

95% go on to higher education studying an increasingly wide range of subjects including law, politics, economics, business studies, languages, mathematics, sciences, information technology, computer studies, psychology, marketing, education, media studies and journalism.

How?

- By being taught by staff who are both subject specialists and qualified in teaching visually impaired students.

- By working in small groups where individual attention and differentiated methods are the norm.

- By achieving independence of spirit through a carefully graded programme of mobility and living skills

- By achieving confidence and pleasure through sports, music, drama, clubs, outings and every kind of outdoor pursuit.

The school is situated on the outskirts of Worcester, on the A44 a mile from Junction 7 of the M5. The centre of the City is within walking distance or there is a bus which passes the College gates.

Applications/selection: Students are assessed for entry at the time and level suitable to them.

For further details please contact Mrs Irene Hodgetts, Liaison Teacher.

RNIB Redhill College

Philanthropic Road, Redhill, Surrey RH1 4DG
Tel: 01737 768935 Fax: 01737 778776
Acting Principal: Judith Foot
Catchment area: Nationwide   Age range: 16-60
Controlled by: RNIB
Fees: FEFC/RT Unit

Provides education, vocational training and rehabilitation of students with a visual impairment.

General description

The College seeks to offer the widest possible choice of innovative, high quality, and appropriate education and training in an enabling and supportive residential setting for people with a visual impairment, with or without other disabilities and learning difficulties, thereby enhancing employability and independence.

The College is situated close to Redhill Station which has good rail links with London and other towns in the south of England. Also close to the M25, M23 and Gatwick Airport.

The College is co-educational and is situated in pleasant grounds in Redhill.

Staffing: In addition to teaching and professional qualifications, all teaching staff are required to take specialist qualifications for teaching the visually-impaired. Teaching staff are recruited from mainstream colleges, business and industry. Residential care staff are similarly required to undertake a special training course run by RNIB.

Students accepted: Visually-impaired adults including younger students (16-20) with learning difficulties, and/or additional disabilities.

Applications/selection: Students are assessed for entry to the course appropriate to them, after application has been made.

Courses and facilities

The College offers a wide range of pre-vocational and vocational courses leading to NVQs and GNVQs. Where appropriate, students may opt for GCSE courses. Opportunities exist for training in administration, horticulture, customer care, IT, computer studies, retail, music, sound recording, remedial therapies and animal care.

The College has a range of specialist teaching provision and residential accommodation in pleasant surroundings.

Links with other establishments

Leisure activities: A wide range of activities are arranged by the Leisure Coordinator including swimming, fitness training and visits to places of entertainment and interest. There is a new fitness centre and exercise pool. The centre is fitted with special adapted equipment suitable for people with disabilities.

RNIB Vocational College

Radmoor Road, Loughborough, Leicestershire, LE11 3BS
Tel: 01509 611077 Fax: 01509 232013
E-mail: gjackman@rnib.org.uk
Principal: Mr K Connell
Catchment area: National   Age range: 16 +
Controlled by: Royal National Institute for the Blind

RNIB Vocational College works with others so that blind and partially-sighted people can develop the skills and personal qualities they need in order to make progress in their lives.

General description

Students are able to follow specialist programmes available at the Vocational College or may follow one of the courses offered by Loughborough College, next door, with specialist support from the Vocational College.

RNIB Vocational College is the only specialist college for blind and partially-sighted people offering residential and day courses in partnership with a mainstream college on the same campus.

Courses and facilities

Loughborough College offers a wide range of courses with intensive support from the RNIB Vocational College. Options range from business studies and information technology to hotel and catering, leisure and tourism and health and social care.

Students receive full support from RNIB Vocational College's visual impairment support service which operates from a resource base within Loughborough College itself. The level of support is on an individual basis depending upon student needs.

RNIB Vocational College offers:

- Foundation course
- employment assessment and work preparation
- IT
- business administration (with the opportunity to focus on either telephony or audio transcription/wordprocessing)
- teleworking course with the opportunity to learn telephone techniques, telemarketing and enterprise skills as well as computer networking.

Students may follow a range of additional modules to complement and support their programme:

- Access learning technologies
- Braille
- Business English and business calculation.

The college also offers short courses to suit individual student needs. Students can also combine options from both colleges, e.g. telephony with languages.

Links with other establishments

External services: RNIB Vocational College's External Services provides support to students at other colleges within the Midlands and also offers short courses and on the job training.

Student services: In support of its students, the RNIB Vocational College offers a range of services including careers education guidance, employment counselling, a low vision clinic, medical services and independent living skills.

Residential accommodation: The college is able to offer students accommodation in its purpose built halls of residence, in houses owned by RNIB in town, and in Loughborough College's halls of residence.

RNID Poolemead

Watery Lane, Twerton on Avon, Bath BA2 1RN.
Tel: 01225 332818
Deputy Director/Head of Poolemead Services: Craig A Crowley
Catchment area: Nationwide   Age range: 18 +
Controlled by: Royal National Institute for Deaf People
Fees: Long term care: Deaf - from £800 per week, deaf-blind - from £900 per week
Rehabilitation: Deaf - from £976 per week. Pennard Court Flats - three levels of rent according to size of flat - costs available on request. DSS local limit payments apply to all rehabilitation and long-term care placements and are deductible from fees

RNID Poolemead aims to provide habilitation and rehabilitation for adult deaf and deaf/blind people with additional disabilities.

General description

Sited on the outskirts of Bath, RNID Poolemead provides rehabilitation as well as long term support for deaf, deaf-blind and deaf multi-disabled adults. Recreation facilities are provided together with the use of local sport and recreation facilities. Pennard Court, in the grounds of RNID Poolemead, contains warden supported flats and there are also four group homes situated in the local community. Real work opportunities are provided via an off-site workshop.

Staffing: 70 full-time residential social workers; twelve instructors in Education and Day Services Unit; local consultant psychiatrist and medical officer; access to other medical facilities; speech therapy and hearing therapy.

Students accepted: Deaf people with multiple physical and mental disabilities. Ability range from learning difficulties to above average. 58 residents, men and women. Day students accepted in the Education and Day Services Unit. Nursing facilities provided.

Applications/selection: Forms from RNID Poolemead. The prospective resident, parents, social workers, teachers etc. are fully involved in the admissions procedure. Waiting periods vary.

Courses and facilities

Each resident is given an individual programme of habilitation or rehabilitation to suit their needs. Programmes are based on total environmental care therapy. Intake frequency dependent on vacancies, but throughout year.

Links with other establishments

As and when necessary.

Robinia
Advantage

Unit 7, Marchington Industrial Estate, Stubby Lane,
Marchington, Uttoxeter, Staffs ST14 8LP
Tel: 01283 829200 Fax: 01283 829201
Website: www.robina.co.uk/
Principal: P Saddington
Catchment area: Nationwide   Age range: Age 16 +
Controlled by: Independent residential establishment
Fees: Details on request

COPE

**General
description**

A project for young people coming out of care/residential schools. Approved training centre. Social Services registered. Approved by the Further Education Funding Council. Fully residential - 41 week placements.

Applications/selection: Further details on request.

**Courses and
facilities**

Individual programmes covering further education, training and work experience to help transition into work and independent living.

Royal National College for the Blind (RNC)

College Road, Hereford HR1 1EB
Enrolment Tel: 01432 370410
Switchboard Tel: 01432 265725   Fax: 01432 353478
Email: md@rncb.ac.uk
Principal: Mrs Roisin Burge
Age range: 16 +
Catchment area: Nationwide & international
Controlled by: Board of Governors. DfEE recognition. Accredited by British Council for Independent Further & Higher Education
Fees: Most places funded by FEFC or the Employment Service

Aims to promote the independence and potential of people who are blind or partially sighted.

General description

The college is situated a mile from the centre of Hereford, with easy access to national rail and bus services. Two main teaching blocks and four halls of residence are set in beautifully maintained grounds. Sports and recreational facilities include a fitness studio, sports hall and social club with licensed/coffee bars. The college's flexible learning centre boasts a wide array of the most up-to-date educational equipment.

Staffing: A total of 170, including 68 teaching staff, the majority holding specialist qualifications in teaching people who have a visual impairment. A large professional care and independence team provides mobility, daily living and social skills, counselling, low vision and welfare advice, 24-hour helpers and medical cover etc.

Students accepted: Blind or partially-sighted, school-leavers and mature students. Students with additional impairments (e.g. hearing impairment, specific learning difficulties, also welcomed).

Applications/selection: Apply to the Registrar. Candidates attend a two-day residential assessment, for which no charge is made.

Courses and facilities

- Access to higher education
- Flexible Foundation (an opportunity to improve basic skills before further study)
- A wide range of GCSEs, A and AS levels
- Foundation in art & design
- GNVQ business studies (Single Award, Intermediate, Foundation and Advanced)
- NVQ administration (levels 2 & 3)
- NVQ information technology (levels 1-2)
- NVQ sport & recreation (levels 1 & 2)
- NVQ in processing information using telecommunications (level 2)
- BTEC First and National Diplomas in performing arts
- BTEC National Diploma in music technology
- VIEW Diploma in piano tuning and repairs
- ITEC Diplomas in aromatherapy, physiology, massage and reflexology
- English as a foreign or second language
- Short courses

Links with other establishments

Some A level students attend Herefordshire College of Technology and other Hereford colleges for certain courses, with tutorial/learning resource support from RNC.

Out-of-term contacts: Linda Wilkes, Registrar.

The Royal School for Deaf Children and Westgate College

Victoria Road, Margate, Kent CT9 1NB
Tel: 01843 227561 (voice and minicom) Fax: 01843 227637
Email: rsdcm@aol.com
Principal: David Bond MA

WESTGATE COLLEGE

St. Gabriel's House, Elm Grove, Westgate-on-Sea, Kent CT8 8LB
Principal: David Bond   Head of College: Freda Brown
Tel: 01843 836300 Fax: 01843 830001
Minicom: 01843 830002
Email: general@westgate-college.org.uk
Age range: 16-25   Member of NATSPEC

The Royal School for Deaf Children was founded in 1792. We are a non-maintained, residential school and college serving Southern England and the Channel Islands. Westgate College for deaf people is our Further Education Department and caters for approximately 50-60 students of either sex. We provide appropriate educational and residential programmes, with the framework of a high quality communication environment. Opportunities are available for further study, vocational training and the development of independent living skills. Students attending Westgate College are usually severely to profoundly deaf, and require signed communication (British Sign Language, Signs Supporting English etc.)

General description

The College is situated away from the main school campus and comprises six pleasant residential and teaching units, ranging from highly-supported living and working environments to student hostels and flats for those requiring less support. We work in collabroration with Thanet and Canterbury FE Colleges where we have teaching bases, and with Hadlow College in Canterbury.

Courses and facilities

Courses are designed to meet the needs of individual students. All courses include a residential curriculum which is planned to increase the student's autonomy, encourage informed decision-making and develop personal and social independence skills. Our courses include:

Externally accredited courses: in colleges of further education, with core skills input, tutorial time and support from a qualified teacher of the deaf, tutors and communication support staff. Staff support for individual or small groups of our students accessing mainstream courses.

Vocational access courses: mainly in colleges of further education. Courses prepare students for external accreditation whilst maintaining a high level of input into areas such as numeracy, literacy and communication. Education about work forms a core component. There are opportunities for real work experience in a variety of placements.

Life experience course – Social Education Programme: for students with significant disabilities in addition to deafness. Every aspect of the student's life is incorporated into an opportunity for learning as part of a 24-hour social education curriculum. All teaching is applied to real life, personally-related experiences in an environment where all communication is signed.

Vocational placements: Vocationally-related education and experience is available to all students according to their needs and abilities. Excellent links with a wide variety of local and national businesses, provide students with the opportunity to learn about and experience the wider world of work. Students receive training and support throughout the whole work experience process.

Sheltered work placements are available for students who are developing pre-vocational skills, but require more time to develop a fuller understanding of the requirements of the open workplace.

Additional information - prospectus, assessment, fees etc. Contact the Head of College.

Royal Schools for the Deaf Manchester

Stanley Road, Cheadle Hulme, Cheadle, Cheshire SK8 6RQ
Tel: 0161 610 0100 Fax: 0161 610 0101
Website: www.rsdmanchester.org
Email: headteacher@rsdmanchester.org
Principal: Mr Leighton Reed
Catchment area: Nationwide   Age range: 5-21
Controlled by: Non-maintained Board of Governors
Fees: £26,000 upwards according to needs

Aims to provide educational and residential provision for hearing-impaired pupils and students with additional complex needs. 52 week placements available. Total communication environment. Differentiated curriculum.

General description

Pleasant buildings on a 30-acre site, south of Manchester on edge of Cheshire Plain. Reasonable access for physically disabled. Separate assessment centre and medical centre. Good access to shops and community facilities. Several minibuses for transport.

Staffing: Teaching: 10 qualified Teachers of the Deaf, 2 qualified MSI, 14 support staff (full-time), 34 intervenor support staff, 28 child care staff, 4 tutors. Multi-disciplinary team consisting of educational psychologist, educational audiologist, physiotherapist, occupational therapist, speech and language therapist (autism specialist). Behaviour Management Team: Head of Care, Assistant Headteacher, psychiatrist, educational psychologist, sign language instructor.

Students accepted: Admission from age 4-19. Students post 19 admitted subject to FEFC funding up to age 21. All pupils have a hearing impairment or communication difficulties requiring an alternative supportive communication system plus additional complex needs: MLD, SLD, PMLD, EBD, challenging behaviour, autism, physical disability and epilepsy.

24 hour consistent curriculum - OFSTED recognised. Investors in People and Positive about Disabled People award holders.

Applications/selection: All pupils/students take part in a week's assessment consisting of school placement and clinical assessment by multi-disciplinary team.

Courses and facilities

All post-16 students have multiple disabilities, with deafness as a common feature. The students, depending on ability both intellectually and socially, are accommodated within two departments - Further Education or Extended Education.

Students entering the departments spend a varying length of time at the Schools. A very small number of students will find employment, even then, realistically, this would be in a sheltered environment, others progress to further study in local colleges or day/residential provision.

The post-16 programme seeks to introduce students to community resources, e.g. colleges, leisure facilities, while giving them the opportunity to sample work placements both on and off the school site. Key Skills continue to be taught but in a functional way linked to a modular programme or through various mini enterprise schemes.

Links with other establishments

With Stockport College of Further and Higher Education, Wythenshawe Technical College, St James Comprehensive School, Greenhayes Centre (Deaf Studies) City College, Manchester, business and community.

Royal West of England College for the Deaf

50 Topsham Road, Exeter, Devon EX2 4NF
Voice & Minicom: 01392 272692 Tel: 01392 215179
Fax: 01392 410016
Head of College: Joyce Hedges
Age range: 16 +
Catchment area: South West, South & South East, South Wales and South Midlands
Controlled by: Non-maintained with DfEE recognition
Fees: On application

Aims to enable hearing-impaired students to develop the practical skills and qualities essential to meet the needs of industry and of life in a hearing world and to equip them with the necessary coping strategies to enable them to play a full part in society.

General description

Students at the college have individual study bedrooms in the main block. More mature students have flats or bedsits on campus. Full range of computing and IT facilities, workshops, own swimming pool and gym. Local sports club used and a variety of outdoor pursuits arranged; sailing dinghies and canoes available with courses run on a regular basis. Students have access to radio hearing aids, minicom phones, fax machines and email.

Staffing: Well qualified tutors include a hearing-impaired tutor for signing and independence training; six communicators; four teaching assistants; eight full-time care officers for resident students; one principal care officer; two student counsellors; educational psychologist; audiologist; speech therapist; school medical officer; physiotherapist; psychiatric counselling.

Students accepted: All types of hearing impairment (including students with additional learning difficulties). Ability range up to A level. Co-educational.

Applications /selection: Application forms, prospectus, and answers to enquiries from the Head of College. Interviews are arranged as applications are received. Yearly entry in September.

Courses and facilities

On site courses include OCNSW Personal Achievement and Communication Course, LCCI Vocational Access Course, C&G 6145 Multiskills, C&G 6135 Basic Woodworking Skills, C&G Wordpower, C&G Numberpower, AEB Basic Literacy and Numeracy, AEB Life Skills, AEB Health & Safety, RSA Wordprocessing, typing, CLAIT, Pitmans Basic Business Skills, NVQ Administration level I, CACDP levels I-III

Sector college courses: A number of students attend Exeter, East Devon and Bicton Colleges. All such students receive Teacher of the Deaf and communicator support in lectures and evening tutorials. Courses include: A levels, GNVQ courses at all levels, NVQs, plus a variety of other courses.

Links with other establishments

Links with Exeter & East Devon Colleges & Bicton College of Agriculture.

Ruskin Mill Further Education Centre

Millbottom, Nailsworth, Gloucestershire GL6 0LA
Tel: 01453 837500   Fax: 01453 835029
Principal: Aonghus Gordon
Catchment area: UK   Age range: 16-25
Fees: FEFC fee bands apply, or by negotiation with Social Services departments

Ruskin Mill Further Education Centre (RMFEC) exists to provide new opportunities for young people who display developmental delay or difficulty. This could take the form of learning difficulties, challenging behaviour, childhood neglect or social sensitivities.

General description

RMFEC, an independent charitable trust, is situated on its own 100 acre site and consists of two converted cloth mills, a small mixed farm, market garden, trout farm, lake and woodland. It is open to the public. There are craft workshops, exhibition and performance space, organic vegetable shop, coffee shop and restaurant.

Staffing: Teaching is done in small groups of not more than four students, or on a 1:1 basis if this is required, by staff qualified in the appropriate craft, landwork, or basic skills area.

The model of residential care at Ruskin Mill is that of a family group with teenage children who are likely to leave home within the next 2-4 years. 25 individual households, located within the local communities, offer a range of care provision, enabling RMFEC to be responsive to the individual needs of the students. Where appropriate students can progress from a highly structured care situation to an experience of independent living in one of the independent living training flats or cottages.

Students accepted: The RMFEC has places for up to 65 students aged between 16 and 25. It has been inspected by the FEFC in 1995 and 1997 and is awarded a Grade 2 standard. The educational and therapeutic approach underpinning the RMFEC is inspired by Rudolf Steiner and William Morris. Some students at the RMFEC have exhibited challenging behaviour and emotional disturbance, others have been unable to form meaningful relationships due to conditions such as Asperger's Syndrome. Often students have been unable to come to terms with the consequences of having a specific learning difficulty, an unusual sensitivity or a delicate constitution.

Application/selection: Applications should be made to the Admissions and Assessments Coordinator, who will arrange visits and discuss the suitability of a placement. Referrals are accepted from prospective students and their carers, careers services, social services departments. Enquiries from others are welcome.

Courses and facilities

Ruskin Mill is a centre for a wide range of accrediting bodies and many elements of the students' individual learning programmes are accredited. Examples include the OCN, RSA, City and Guilds, NCFE and AQA. GCSE and A level courses are available where appropriate. Students are able to progress to NVQ or equivalent vocational qualifications both at Ruskin Mill and through integration into local colleges. Students take part in individual programmes designed to enable them to make the most of their own potential. Therapeutic craft activities, basic and continuing education, work experience within the RMFEC's own small businesses and vocational training are all available. Social and interpersonal skills are developed through: 1:1 counselling and therapy sessions; small intensive groups working together in the craft workshops and on the land; group work in drama, story telling and music; regular educational and recreational visits to the continent.

Links with other establishments

RMFEC has links with local colleges, crafts people, businesses and the wider community. See above for further details.

St Catherine's School

Grove Road, Ventnor, Isle of Wight, PO38 1TT
Tel: 01983 852722   Fax: 01983 857219
Website: www.stcatherines.org.uk
Email: stcaths@onthepc.co.uk
Principal: G E Shipley
Catchment area: UK and overseas   Age range: 8-19
Controlled by: Board of Governors
Fees: 1999/2000 £23,451

The aims of St Catherine's school are: to provide a sound general education. To provide, through a multi-disciplinary team approach, a total language environment for each pupil. To provide each pupil with a programme of education designed to meet individual needs and abilities and, where necessary, to provide intensive speech therapy. To teach pupils the necessary skills to overcome or cope successfully with their difficulties, so that if possible they can return to their homes and mainstream schools. To equip senior pupils with the effective lifeskills, qualifications and confidence they will need when they leave school. To provide a calm, friendly atmosphere in order to build confidence and mutual respect and to encourage progress in all pupils/students.

General description

St Catherine's School, Ventnor, is a residential special school for pupils with primary speech and language disorders. St Catherine's is recognised and approved by the DfEE as a special school for the education of pupils with special educational needs. The school is established as a company limited by guarantee with charitable status, conducted by a Board of Governors and an appointed Principal.

Staffing: Nine full-time and three part-time teachers; eight full-time speech and language therapists; six ancillaries; 20 care staff and one nurse.

Students accepted: Students with disorders of speech and language.

Applications/selection: To the Principal. Up-to-date reports required from: the school, speech therapist, educational psychologist and medical officer.

Courses and facilities

St Catherine's offers pre-vocational courses and ASDAN Youth Award for a group of mixed sex students taught in a separate building. The course makes use of the local college of further education and the local community. Students continue to receive intensive speech therapy and specific language remediation programmes. Separate living accommodation provides the opportunity for increasing independence to prepare each student for life after school.

Links with other establishments

Links with local High School, Middle School and the Isle of Wight College of Arts & Technology.

St Christopher's School

Aims to prepare the pupils to find their place in the world, either in a sheltered environment or in the wider community.

General description

Founded in 1945, the School is ideally located on the edge of Durdham Downs. The proximity of the city is a great advantage - both for leisure activities and social development. There are six hostels, of various sizes, catering for the differing age groups and needs. Leisure activities, including minibus outings and use of the school pool, are an integral part of hostel life. A Christian service is held on Sundays when all pupils attend. A wholefood, additive-free diet is provided where possible, and maximum use is made of organic vegetables. Art is an integral part of education - drawing, painting, modelling and drama enhances the pupil's experience of life. Music sessions take place daily in each class and a weekly school concert is given by teachers and pupils. There is provision for children on 52 week placement.

Staffing: Qualified medical staff are on duty day and night to give help and advice when necessary. Homeopathic remedies are used where possible.

Students accepted: Children with severe learning difficulties, some also with challenging behaviour, some with mobility difficulties.

Applications/selection: Contact the Educational Registrar at the above address.

Courses and facilities

Pupils are educated over a six-term year in small classes with a high staff ratio. The curriculum is based on the principles of curative education indicated by Rudolf Steiner for children with special needs. Pupils also have access to the National Curriculum, independence and social skills and a range of therapies. Pupils aged 14-19 have access to ASDAN accreditation schemes.

St Davids Care in the Community

Fairfield, St Davids Road, St Davids Pembs SA62 6QH
Tel: 01437 720003 Fax: 01437 720175
Email: sdavidcare@aol.com
Age range: 18 upwards
Catchment area: No restriction
Fees: Variable according to needs. Rising annually

St Davids Care in the Community is a residential community providing education as well as life placements to individuals with moderate to severe learning disabilities. Our aim is to provide clients with an increasing level of learning and activities which enable them to develop individually to the optimum of their ability.

General description

Life in our 'community' is based on a progression of nine group homes, each with its own homely atmosphere and a strong sense of 'family' amongst the residents. Clients can progress from fully-supported accommodation to independent living in their own flats. We are situated within the smallest city in the country - St Davids, in the heart of Pembrokeshire Coast National Park.

Staffing: We employ 34 care and education staff.

Students accepted: Age 18+ on admission, male and female. Moderate to severe learning disabilities; a few placements for physical/mental disability. Currently 47 clients.

Applications: Enquiries direct to St Davids Care in the Community.

Courses and facilities

Whilst we offer a full range of further education programme in literacy, numeracy and social and life skills, learning also takes place outside the Community. We offer realistic work experience on our two farms, in our restaurant, gardens and greenhouses, arts and craft rooms, and in domestic services.

Each student has an individual programme, tailor-made to their level of ability, with regular assessments and progress recorded by highly qualified and experienced staff. Courses in horticulture, animal husbandry, agriculture, and general skills are accredited through the National Proficiency Tests Council and the Welsh Joint Education Committee.

St Elizabeth's School

South End, Much Hadham, Hertfordshire SG10 6EW
Tel: 01279 843451   Fax: 01279 843903
Acting Headteacher: Sr Patricia Ainsworth
Age range: 5-19+
Catchment area: National - with regional bias
Controlled by: Congregation of the Daughters of the Cross;
DfEE recognition
Fees: 1999/2000 starting at £45,384

Aims to provide individual education/training programmes for young people with special needs, to enable each of them to achieve as many areas of independence and fulfilment as possible, leading to as fully an integrated life in society as possible.

General description

St Elizabeth's is situated on the edge of the large village of Much Hadham, six miles out of Bishops Stortford, and eight miles from Stansted Airport. The facility for 16-19 year olds is part of a larger centre, primarily for people with epilepsy. School for 50+ 5-16 year olds. Residential units and educational training facilities for approximately 90 adult residents. Set within 60 acres of farmland, St Elizabeth's has a wide range of support services; comprehensive medical supervision, physiotherapy, speech therapy, riding for the disabled, swimming for the disabled, an interested and supportive local community. Regular clubs on and off site. Hobbies, etc. encouraged. Theatre and cinema outings.

Staffing: Teaching staff and ancillary workers, educational psychologist, nursing staff, physiotherapist; speech therapist, residential social workers, CSVs and regular voluntary help from local area. Level of support varies with individual students. Three epilepsy clinics on site weekly. Additional clinics with neurologist, paediatrician, psychiatrist.

Students accepted: Adolescents with epilepsy and associated problems who have learning difficulties, moderate/severe. Students with other disabilities who would benefit from the specialised facilities, eg physical, sensory, emotional or social disabilities. Although fully ramped, cannot accept severely physically disabled. Blind or deaf students would not usually be accepted. 26 residential places, mixed sex, some day placements.

Applications/selection: If not transferring from main school, a day's interview/ assessment on receipt of completed application forms. Application forms available from the Headteacher. Informal visits may be arranged prior to seeking sponsorship.

Courses and facilities

Usual stay three years. Programmes designed to meet the individual's needs and abilities.

City & Guilds Foundation Level, RSA + ASDAN and CPVE courses arranged to suit individual needs.

Lifeskills training: communication - independence - are the core of the whole course. Throughout their stay, students will participate in selected parts of the support curriculum which includes: numeracy, literacy, budgeting, purchasing, home economics, storing (food & equipment), kitchen duties, domestic duties, rural studies, gardening, animal husbandry, horticulture, home decorating, household furnishings, CDT, IT, DIY, general home maintenance, art and craft, music and drama, health education, badminton, tennis, keep fit, typing, office and reception duties.

Links with other establishments

Community service: work experience (on and off site) arranged if student is ready for this experience.

St John's College

Walpole Road, Brighton, East Sussex BN2 2AF
Tel: 01273 244000
Principal: Mike Hudson
Catchment area: None defined   Age range: 14-19
Controlled by: Trustees and Governors (Non-maintained special school)
Fees: Sliding scale dependent on the needs of the student

Aims for students to achieve as much independence as possible by the end of their course. Aims to assess future needs for placement and training and to liaise with accepting authorities.

General description

St John's is a non-maintained special college catering for boys and girls, most of whom have moderate or severe learning difficulties. Most have additional medical, behavioural or communication difficulties.

Staffing: Fully qualified teaching staff, very experienced classroom assistants, speech therapist, physiotherapist, counsellor, RGN nursing cover. Staff/pupil 4:1.

Students accepted: Moderate and severe learning difficulties. Controlled epileptics, communication difficulties, autism.

Applications/selection: To the Principal, copy of latest statement and report from specialist careers officer. Medical and psychological reports.

Courses and facilities

1. Extension course, Lewes Technical College.

2. Extension course, Brighton College of Technology.

In both colleges there are opportunities for students to attend other courses if appropriate.

3. St John's College.

Courses include Wordpower, Numberpower, Further Education Award, NVQ level I, GCSE, AEB, ASDAN Towards Independence.

New residential provision recently completed.

Links with other establishments

Brighton College of Technology, Lewes Technical College and Plumpton Agricultural College.

St Joseph's Extended Education Unit

Stratford Lawn, Stroud, Gloucestershire GL5 4AP
Tel: 01453 763793 Fax: 01453 752617
Principal: Sr M Quentin OP, BA
Catchment area: National   Age range: 16-19
Controlled by: Board of Governors: St Roses School
Fees: On application

Aims to continue and consolidate basic education and to enable young people to appreciate their personal worth and become as independent as possible.

General description

The house is quite separate from the main school and accommodation is in single or double rooms. It is situated in the town of Stroud with easy access to shops, Post Office, banks, leisure centre, etc. Facilities available in the house for students to do their own cooking and washing. Purpose built workshop for leisure pursuits and work experience.

Staffing: One senior teacher; one assistant teacher; one occupational therapist; one workshop instructor; one physiotherapist; six special support assistants; one nurse; GP at Medical Centre; visiting orthopaedic consultant; admin staff and cleaners, etc.

Students accepted: 13 students, boys and girls, who have difficulties arising from their physical problems, except severe behavioural disorders. Facilities also for students with visual impairment as well as physical disability.

Applications/selection: Informal contact welcomed. Official application through local education authority as early as possible. For information please contact Mr Philip Medlow.

Courses and facilities

Each student has his or her own individual programme according to need. This includes basic numeracy, literacy, social studies, social skills, cookery, laundry, all of which can lead to a number of qualifications such as: Youth Award Scheme (FE and Towards Independence), Wordpower, Numberpower and Preliminary Cookery Certificate. In addition to this, students have the opportunity to take AEB Basic Tests and RSA/Pitman information technology examinations. Some students attend local schools and technical colleges for certain subjects and social events. Courses last one to three years according to need, and at the end of that time it is hoped that students will have gained sufficient maturity and independence to benefit from further education in an FE college or specialised college.

Links with other establishments

Close liaison is maintained with mainstream schools and colleges. Work experience organised locally whenever appropriate and possible.

St Joseph's School

Amlets Lane, Cranleigh, Surrey GU6 7DH
Tel: 01483 272449 Fax: 01483 276003
Principal: Mr A Lowry
Catchment area: South of England   Age range: 7-19 +
Controlled by: R.C. Diocese of Arundel and Brighton
Fees: Residential: £27,400 Day £18,320

The course has a broad and balanced curriculum which fosters autonomy, increases independence and confidence in preparing students for an adult life which will enable them to assume new roles both within the family and the community.

General description

St Joseph's is placed on the outskirts of Cranleigh 10 miles from Guildford.

Residential group houses are situated both on the campus and within the local community.

Staffing: The course has its own co-ordinator and is overseen by the head of education and linked through the 14-19 curriculum to the pre-sixteen department: staff teach in both departments. The course has access to the services of three qualified speech and language therapists and two qualified nurses. Seven learning support assistants work specifically with the students on this course.

Students accepted: 30 mixed. Moderate/severe learning difficulties and those with communication and language disorders. The school provides physiotherapy and occupational therapy to those students assessed as being in need.

Applications/selection A familiarisation period is offered to students whose needs are likely to be met.

Courses and facilities

Individualised programmes for students of two to three years duration. The course runs on 24 hour curriculum principles. Programmes of study include: community skills, travel skills, home management skills, work-related activities including work experience, sport and leisure activities, communication skills, numeracy and literacy support, creative and expressive arts, and personal and social and health education. The skills and knowledge learnt within these programmes are nationally accredited by RSA, NSP, ALL, ASDAN, OCR, NEAB.

Students receive an accredited updated NRA on leaving, have the opportunity to work towards the Duke of Edinburgh Award and take part in a yearly residential activity week.

Out-of-term contact: The office is open mornings during school holidays.

St Loye's College (Assessment & Development Centre)

Fairfield House, Topsham Road, Exeter, Devon EX2 6EP
Tel: 01392 255428 Fax: 01392 420889
Principal: Miss M E Peat
Catchment area: Nationwide   Age range: 18 +
Controlled by: Board of Management, St Loye's Foundation - Chief Executive: Mr David Imber
Fees: Details of fees through the Admissions Officer

Provides assessment, work preparation and foundation training, and intensive tuition in literacy, numeracy and basic vocational skills to enable people with special training needs to enter vocational training courses at the college or to obtain appropriate placement elsewhere.

General description

Situated on the outskirts of Exeter in an attractive rural setting. In addition to its Assessment and Development Centre, the Foundation operates vocational training and a school of Health Studies. There is excellent single accommodation and a wide range of sports and recreational facilities.

Staffing: The Assessment and Development Centre is an integral part of St Loye's College with an instructional staff of six, together with full care and medical cover.

Students accepted: People of all ages with physical disabilities who need to identify and overcome barriers to vocational progress. Such barriers could be poor literacy and numeracy; long-term unemployment; the absence of work experience; the need for wider experience of skills; the lack of confidence and other factors which have prevented satisfactory completion of an appropriate vocational training programme.

Application/selection: Applications through DSTs. For further details contact Paul Collings (Admissions Officer) on 01392 255428/01392 286208.

St Piers

> St Piers Lane, Lingfield, Surrey RH7 6PW
> Tel: 01342 832243 Fax: 01342 834639
> Chief Executive: Bob Haug   FE Principal: Mrs Christine Davies
> Medical director: Dr F M C Besag
> Admissions Coordinator: Mandy Snelling
> Catchment area: National   Age range: 5-19 +
> Controlled by: Independent body of Managers; DfEE approved, FEFC inspected
> Fees: Five tier system. Please contact Admissions for details

COPE

Aims to enable young people with epilepsy and other neurological disorders to enjoy a full role within society by providing each individual with the highest standards of integrated education, medical attention and residential care.

General description

Set in over 100 acres of pleasant countryside in Surrey, close to the Kent and Sussex borders. St Piers maintains a variety of recreational facilities including a heated indoor swimming pool, a full size sports hall and outdoor pursuits centre.

Students live in hostels within the grounds, and are encouraged to take an active part in the running of their hostels. Hostels provide programmes of independent living and social skills training as an integral part of the 24 hour curriculum.

Staffing: In addition to teaching and residential care teams, there are doctors, psychologists, speech and language therapists, occupational therapists and physiotherapists. Each student has a named Key Worker and a Personal Tutor.

Applications/selection: Informal enquiries are welcome and should be through the Admissions Coordinator, on 01342 831243.

Formal applications should be made via the local education authorities which are normally responsible for fees, or for initiating an application for funding from the FEFC. Following a formal application and an informal visit, prospective students will be considered for a two-day assessment leading to a possible placement.

Courses and facilities

Entry into St Piers Further Education can be negotiated from the age of 16. Students commence their studies by undertaking a one-term foundation programme following which an individual education programme is negotiated.

Courses available: ASDAN Working towards Independence, Youth Award Scheme bronze/silver, City & Guilds Wordpower, Numberpower, National Proficiency Test Council Vocational Foundation modules including horticulture, animal care, independent living skills, vehicle preparation, workshop practice, literacy, numeracy and communication, information technology.

Open college accredited programmes are also offered in all of the above plus textiles, home management, music and creative arts, design technology, sports & recreation.

There is a thriving business administration and office skills department offering a range of programmes from foundation level through to NVQ level 2/3. NVQ level 1/2 is offered in information technology and in land based industries.

The curriculum includes sport & recreation and creative arts; both areas seek to introduce students to community facilities and activities. Students are also offered the opportunity to undertake work experience both on and off site.

Links with other establishments

St Piers is a member of the Tandridge Consortium for school & colleges. St Piers works closely with local sector colleges including East Surrey, Crawley, Brinsbury College and Oxted County Sixth Form. Local employers, including National Westminster, BAA Gatwick and The Open University, provide work experience placements.

SCOPE Thorngrove Centre

> Mulberry Court, Common Mead Lane, Gillingham, Dorset SP8 4RE
> Tel: 01747 822241/2 Fax: 01747 825966
> Manager: Mr N Bond
> Age range: 18 +
> Catchment area: National
> Controlled by: SCOPE
> Fees: Based on individual assessment

Aims to provide residential accommodation for people with cerebral palsy, who also wish to contribute to the running of our garden centre.

General description

Thorngrove Garden Centre is pleasantly situated in 50 acres of farmland near the town of Gillingham, Dorset. It has a large and modern glasshouse nursery producing houseplants, bedding plants and shrubs to the general public.

Staffing: 16 staff including care workers, horticultural instructors, visiting social worker and other support staff.

Residents accepted: 17 male & female with cerebral palsy, ambulant or semi-ambulant.

Applications/selection: Application in the first instance to the Manager. Informal visits welcomed followed by short stay for assessment. Variable waiting times for admission. It is expected that a local authority assessment will have been completed and funding agreed.

Courses and facilities

Mulberry court provides accommodation for 10 people, in two purpose built bungalows which are staffed continually.

We have three other community homes where service users live more independently, but are provided with agreed staff input and 24-hour backup from Mulberry Court for emergencies.

The service comprises a team of staff offering support using individual plans so that each person can develop in the way that suits them best. Practical help and encouragement for those wishing to live more independently. Leisure activities include swimming, horse riding, yoga, group holidays and outings, and a wide range of hobbies such as photography, sport and cookery.

The Garden Centre gives service users the opportunity to contribute to the running of a modern plant centre, producing houseplants, shrubs, conifers and bedding plants.

Out-of-term contact: Open all year.

| **Searchlight Workshops** | Claremont Road, Mount Pleasant, Newhaven, East Sussex BN9 0NG |

Tel: 01273 514007 Fax: 01273 611289

Chief Executive: David Bray

Catchment area: UK   Age range: 18 +

Controlled by: Independent Management Committee (East Sussex County Council Registered Home Inspectorate)

Fees: Annual average £20,000

Aims to provide long term care, full-time occupational therapy and work related activities. (Picture framing, badge making, packing, cane work and garden furniture production).

General description

Searchlight Workshops and accommodation are located overlooking the sea in a residential housing estate, offering single or shared rooms. DSS sponsorship.

Staffing: 51 staff including 27 carers.

Students accepted: Males and females with physical and mental disabilities.

Applications/selection: Applications in writing, or phone enquiries to the Chief Executive.

Courses and facilities

Residents are encouraged to pursue whatever hobbies or interests they wish, with some residents attending adult further education courses, e.g. gardening, art etc.

Searchlight has its own social club, with bingo, quizzes, treasure hunts, dances and paying bar. Outings are frequently arranged using one of the specially-adapted buses.

Links with other establishments

Adult further education centre, access committee, East Sussex Association for the Disabled, Federation of Sussex Industries, ESCC Care Home Advisory Committee, The National Association of Industries for the Blind and Disabled etc.

seeAbility

56-66 Highlands Road, Leatherhead, Surrey KT22 8NR.
Tel: 01372 373086 Fax: 01372 370143
Website: www.seeability.org
Chief Executive: Robert Perkins
Catchment area: Nationwide   Age range: 18 +
Controlled by: Trustees
Fees: Payable by Social Services and/or Health Authorities

Working with adults who are visually impaired and have other disabilities, seeAbility aims to explore their potential, develop their skills/ independence and/or enhance the quality of their lives.

General description

Registered charity, founded as Royal School for the Blind, services offered by seeABILITY include: assessment, community outreach, visual impairment rehabilitation, day care, sheltered employment services and residential/nursing services. Additionally, consultancy and training services are offered to carers/other professionals.

Staffing: Social workers, experienced care staff, nurses, rehabilitation workers for the visually impaired, specialist tutors, therapists, counsellor.

Courses and facilities

Residential services are offered at differing levels according to individual need and range from semi-independent living in community based flats/houses to 24 hour staffed accommodation. Visual impairment rehabilitation services include mobility, orientation and daily living skills.

Day services include a wide range of educational, creative and physical activities, both in groups and on an individual basis. Currently operating from Surrey, Sussex, Hampshire and South East London, seeAbility aims to develop service provision in localities throughout London and the South of England.

New services and developments include:

- **Seaford, Sussex** - A residential home for seven young adults with a visual impairment and other disabilities, together with two independent flats, an activity centre and an outreach service. Opened February 1999.

- **Tadley, Hampshire** - A residential nursing home for 16 young adults with a visual impairment and a degenerative illness such as Juvenile Batten's. The accommodation consists of two eight-bedded bungalows and an activity and resources centre. Opened July 1999.

- **Wellington, Somerset** - A residential home for seven young adults with a visual impairment and profound multiple disabilities, together with a resource centre. Due to open autumn 2000.

- **Fleet, Hampshire** – A residential service for eight adults with a visual impairment and other disabilities. Services will encourage individuals to develop their level of independence and to access community resources. Opened January 2000.

For further information or to pursue a referral, please contact Sue Ogden - Placement Manager. Email: s.ogden@seeability.org

Sense East

72 Church Street, Market Deeping, Peterborough, Cambridgeshire PE6 8AL.
Tel: 01778 344921 Fax: 01778 380078
Email: enquiries@senseeast.org.uk
Regional Director: G Roulstone
Catchment area: Nationwide   Age range: 16+
Controlled by: SENSE
Fees: £60,000 per annum

Education and training of students with Rubella Syndrome and multi-sensory impairments.

General description

The Sense East further education service provides 52-week residential education and training. Students live in groups of between three and five in ten different staffed houses in Market Deeping, Peterborough, Skegness and Louth. Ample transport enables easy access to sport, leisure and cultural facilities in surrounding towns and countryside. There is a swimming pool, music room and well-equipped teaching rooms, each with a computer. Vocational training takes place in pottery, woodwork and jewellery-making etc., in craft workshops on local industrial estates.

Staffing: Social tutors (including waking night staff); education tutors; vocational tutors; ancillary and administration staff.

Students accepted: Students with Rubella Syndrome. Students with dual or single sensory impairment, who may have additional learning difficulties, physical disabilities and language delay.

Applications/selection: Telephone/letter to Regional Director in first instance.

Courses and facilities

Individually-designed programmes in areas of communication (including, where appropriate, sign-supported English, Braille and other systems), basic skills in literacy and numeracy, science and creative arts, physical education and independence skills and vocational training.

Links with other establishments

Various courses as part of the training programmes take place at local colleges of further education and other community-based facilities.

Sense West

The Princess Royal Centre, 4 Church Road, Edgbaston, Birmingham B15 3TD
Tel: 0121 687 1564 Fax: 0121 687 1656
Regional Director: Steve Alexander
Age range: 16 +
Catchment area: Midlands & South West
Controlled by: Sense
Fees: On application

Aims to provide developmental services appropriate to the needs of people of all ages with dual sensory impairment and additional learning difficulties and sensory impairments and additional disabilities.

General description

Sense West provides a range of living accommodation designed to meet personal preferences and individual needs. Every effort is made to ensure new schemes blend with the local neighbourhood and are designed to maximise independence, skill development and convey a positive image. The centre aims to offer living environments that recognise the individual needs of each person and seek to provide opportunities, challenges and support that allow each person to be proactive in determining their preferred lifestyle.

Operational policies, staffing levels and lifestyles within each scheme are determined by the preferences and needs of the unique mix of residents.

All accommodation is specifically adapted to allow the sensory impaired person to access, understand and therefore control as much of their immediate world as possible. Use of high colour contrasts, textured surfaces, modified lighting and acoustics help maximise use of residual vision and hearing and enhance mobility and independence.

Each resident has an individual programme that utilises both daily living experiences and specialist resources to provide continuous learning. Planning, structure and consistency ensure all experiences and activities are learning opportunities. All programmes are quality assured. Vocational opportunities are provided as appropriate.

To ensure all environments promote choice and improvement, staff are trained in the principles of deaf-blind education. The approach utilises a specialist form of communication and stresses consistency, structure, predictability and clarity of information.

Other services offered by Sense West include advisory, education and day services, training and consultancy, communicator-guide service and intervenor service.

Staffing: Education team, residential team, support staff and training department.

Students accepted: There is no fixed upper limit. Sensory impaired people with additional learning/physical disabilities. Open 52 weeks a year.

Applications/selection: Contact Krystyna Cieslik - Referral Officer. Upon receipt of forms, visits to the centre from parents and sending authority. Visit from centre to applicant's home and any other relevant establishment.

Courses and facilities

The centre does not offer a specific course as such, but, after an initial assessment period, students are placed on individual programmes which are designed to develop their levels of independence, both within the home and within the local community.

Development of communication skills is one of the most important aspects of the curriculum and this is developed across all areas of activity. Facilities are available for developing the use of vision and hearing where there is potential, and for developing the skills of the totally deaf and blind person. Sense West offers long-term placements but is also keen to work with local authorities in providing long-term accommodation which is suitable for the student.

Links with other establishments

Links are established with the local disabled and able community and with the national service for the deaf-blind.

The Sheiling Community

The Sheiling School, Horton Road, Ashley, Ringwood, Hants
BH24 2EB
Tel/fax: 01425 478680   Email: sheilingco@aol.com
Age range: 6-19   Term: 38 weeks

The Lantern Community, Folly Farm Lane, Ringwood, Hants
BH24 2NN
Tel: 01425 479926 Fax: 01425 471841
Email: lanterncom@aol.com
Age range: 19+   Term: 52 weeks

Sturts Farm Community, Three Cross Road, West Moors,
Ferndown, Dorset BH22 0NF
Tel: 01202 875275 Fax: 01202 891623
Age range: 19+   Term 52 weeks

Catchment area: Unrestricted

Fees: Vary according to which activity is being applied for –
prices on application

Aims to provide further education and practical training within the setting of an integrated therapeutic community, where the unfolding of individual human potential and social integration is complementary to the acquisition of skills.

General description

The Sheiling Community is set in a 50 acre wooded estate and comprises a school (children and senior students to age 19)and the Lantern Community (companions 19+). The students and companions live in family houses together with full-time resident helpers (co-workers) some of whom have families and children of their own. Sturts Farm near West Moors has 90 acres of land. 25 acres are cultivated for vegetables, cereals and fruit, the rest supports a variety of farm animals including two working horses. All the land is farmed productively using traditional methods and without resource to chemicals or fertilisers. There is also a food processing workshop. The philosophy that forms the basis of both the educational work and the striving community is inspired by Rudolf Steiner (1861-1925) whose teachings open up an understanding of the spiritual nature of man in the world. The Christian festivals are celebrated by the community.

Staffing: The resident staff (co-workers) live and work together with the students and companions. They receive no wage but work in answer to the needs of the community. Personal requirements are met according to individual needs and each co-worker is encouraged to develop a sense of involvement and responsibility.

Students accepted: Male and female. Mobile and sighted with special needs/learning difficulties.

Applications/selection: Through the Community's Medical Officer.

Courses and facilities

In addition to the physically demanding agricultural and horticultural work on the land, there is also more sheltered training in woodwork, shopkeeping, food processing and homecare. The practical work is balanced by a curriculum of further education in a wide variety of subjects. Recreational facilities include swimming, folk dancing, courses in art/crafts and participation in the rich cultural life of the community which includes the preparation of plays, pageants and concerts to celebrate the Christian Festivals and seasons of the year. All of these activities are pursued, not for the disabled members of the community but with them. Helper and helped live and work side by side, each contributing towards the well-being of the community according to ability and experience.

Links with other establishments

The Friends of the Sheiling Community who actively support its work through opening up a wider range of social contact and also through volunteer work on a one-to-one basis to improve basic ability in reading and writing. The Community is also closely linked with the wider Association of Camphill Communities.

Contact: Mrs Susan Smith (PR/Liaison Administrator) 01425 478680.

Solden Hill House

Banbury Road, Byfield, Daventry, Northamptonshire NN11 6UA
Tel: 01327 260234
Manager: Ms A O'Hare
Catchment area: UK   Age range: 19 +
Controlled by: Independent
Fees: £577 per week

General description

An independently-run home on Rudolf Steiner principles. Activities include craft work to develop latent skills which are also of therapeutic value. Includes some further education and gardening work. Open for 48 weeks of the year.

Staffing: 19 full-time and ten part-time staff.

Students accepted: Up to 31 young men and women with learning difficulties.

Applications/selection: Apply to the Manager for details and interview.

Links with other establishments

Through Committee for Steiner Education. Member of British Federation of Care Home Proprietors.

Somerset Court

Harp Road, Brent Knoll, Highbridge, Somerset TA9 4HQ
Tel: 01278 760555
Manager: Mr A Duckworth
Age range: 18 +

Aims to provide adult development and care programmes for adults with autism centred around the provision of an emotionally secure and structured pattern of life experiences and opportunities.

General description

Set up in 1974 as the first residential centre in England to cater exclusively for the needs of adults with autism. Somerset Court is a large house with 26 acres used for cultivation of vegetables and produce/plants for sale in the garden centre.

Residents live in family groups in six individual houses, where the aim is to make life for residents as much as possible like living in their own home, looking after themselves and each day going out to work, as well as enjoying planned leisure activities together. Daily activities follow a realistic work-based programme that is service-user orientated. This provides a therapeutic and constructive use of time and encourages independence, self confidence and personal skill development in individual and social functioning. The specific impairments of the condition are challenged in specialised activities.

Staffing: Residential services offer professional care, domestic and leisure activities and individual skills training. Enhanced staffing ratios, usually an average base-line of 1:3. Staff training is seen as an essential component in overall service quality and regular in-service courses are run in conjunction with other professional training agencies.

Students accepted: Up to 44 adults for the residential service with a limited number of day placements.

Courses and facilities

Each resident has a personalised care/activity programme which is determined at annual case conference and subject to ongoing assessment and review through the IPP system.

Subjects include:

- **woodwork** - making toys, household items, garden furniture, seed boxes, trellis etc

- **horticulture** - producing plants, hanging baskets, growing vegetables

- **imaginative development** - producing hand-woven garments, cushions and rugs, focusing on planning, sequencing, cause & effect, and predicting

- **printing** - filling orders for tickets, business cards, stationery, invitation cards, and local magazines

- **grounds maintenance** - maintaining extensive grounds, lawns, shrubberies and flower beds

- **music** - singing, handbell ringing, piano tuition

- **communication** - a wide range of communication-based activity centred on individuals

- **social interaction and development** - including frequent and regular real situation work and presence in the local community

Programmes are focused on ordinary adult values with day, residential and night services providing an integrated care package designed to meet individual need. Full use is made of individual service programmes and keyworkers' assessments in a comprehensive planning and development programme for each individual. The values of home life are embraced and implemented in everyday activities.

Strathmore House, Florence Villa and High Cross House

27 Queens Park Avenue, Dresden, Stoke-on-Trent, Staffordshire ST3 4AU
Tel/fax: 01782 313508
Principals: Ms K Smith & Mr V A Heath
Catchment area: Nationwide
Controlled by: Registered with Social Services
Fees: 1999/2000 £262 - £545 per week 52 week placement

Aims to provide residential training in urban living and independence skills for school-leavers and young adults with special needs. Both long-term and short-term residents accommodated.

General description

All three properties are in pleasant residential areas of the potteries town of Longton. They are within a short walking distance of each other and the town centre.

Staffing: Both proprietors are qualified teachers, experienced in teaching special needs. Also staff qualified and experienced in training/care/residential work.

Students accepted: Most residents have moderate/severe learning difficulties. People with severe physical disabilities not catered for. All three properties function as residential homes and training colleges. We can therefore cater for permanent residency or training residency. We also have two training centres, Jasmine's Florist/Confectionery and Bio 2000 - a manufacturing unit.

Applications/selection By application form. Clients/students referred by careers officers, social workers, health authority workers and parents.

Courses and facilities

Students do not take prescribed courses. Individual programmes are devised to meet their needs. Emphasis is placed on independence training. Where appropriate, training programmes may include work experience. Students are encouraged to use community facilities, swimming baths, leisure centres, youth clubs, special olympic activities, local cinemas, etc. Awarded Grade 1 (for the second time in 1999) by FEFC Inspectorate.

Links with other establishments

Local college of FE, local businesses, registered with Staffordshire Social Services and Staffordshire Association of Registered Homes and ARC.

Out-of-term contact: Operates 52 week year.

Stroud Court Community Trust

Longfords, Minchinhampton, Stroud, Gloucestershire GL6 9AN
Tel: 01453 834020
Executive Director: Lyn Kaminski
Age range: 16 +
Catchment area: Gloucestershire and neighbouring counties.

Stroud Court Community Trust is committed to the continual drive towards excellence on behalf of adults with autism.

General description

The Stroud Court Service - our aims and objectives:

- to create meaningful choices for each individual
- to assist each person in accessing open society
- to exceed minimum legislative standards
- to meet the personal needs of each individual
- to constantly improve and develop the service.

For further information please contact Maria McClarkin, PA to Executive Director.

Taurus Crafts

The Old Park, Lydney, Gloucestershire, GL15 6BU
Tel: 01594 844841 Fax: 01594 845636
Website: www.tauruscrafts.co.uk
Email: training@tauruscrafts.co.uk
Catchment area: Nationwide   Age range: 19 +

COPE

Taurus Crafts is a working community designed to create the opportunity for a broad range of individuals with special needs to gain experience, develop confidence and, when attainable, a qualification, within a commercial environment. We also provide work experience and day-care. Taurus Crafts is part of the Camphill Village Trust.

General description

Taurus is an attempt to establish a new kind of community focused around the workplace. It is envisaged as a viable community enterprise managed for social results. It aims to create opportunities for people whose needs are not well served by mainstream provision. Taurus can provide placements and vocational training in real work situations at Taurus Crafts or with individuals and companies working with Taurus.

Open to the public since August 1995, Taurus Crafts is a growing visitor attraction and craft centre in the Forest of Dean. The centre is based in an old coach house and farm buildings on the Lydney Park Estate just off the A48 between Lydney and Aylburton. The centre encompasses a cafe restaurant, pottery, craft shop and other workshops.

Accommodation can be arranged for trainees with local families or in small residential homes for a fee. The training fee varies from £6.50 per hour to £128.50 a week.

Staffing: Taurus Crafts has a team of staff and volunteers with wide experience in their professional areas and experience of working with people with special needs.

Trainees: Depending on funding, the centre can provide up to 20 training, work experience and day care places. Female and male trainees accepted. They can be people with special needs i.e. learning disabilities, people with mental health problems or people with physical disabilities, although the whole operation is not accessible to people with significant mobility disabilities.

Application/selection: Please apply direct to Taurus Crafts. If we are in the position to provide a training place, a placement assessment will be organised to confirm the offer of training and develop a customised training programme.

Courses and facilities

The 'trainees' are placed in a real working environment at Taurus Crafts. The project seeks to provide, as appropriate to the trainee, skills training and work experience, the opportunity for growing independence in the working environment, placement in sheltered employment and transfer to paid employment. Taurus Crafts currently offers training and work experience in the following areas; catering, pottery, retail, horticulture and office administration and is willing to try and organise training around particular craft skills through local craft workers if possible. The centre is recognised by the National Proficiency Testing Council.

Links with other establishments

The centre has close links with the Grange and Oaklands, two neighbouring Camphill Village communities. The centre also works closely with the local further education college.

Templehill Community

Glenfarquhar Lodge, Auchenblae, Laurencekirk, Kincardineshire AB30 1UJ
Tel: 01561 320230 Fax: 01561 320283
Website: www.camphillscotland.org.uk
Email: templehill@compuserve.com
Coordinator: Mr R S Keys B.A.
Age range: 16-25+
Controlled by: Templehill Community Ltd, a registered charity
Member of the Association of Camphill Communities
Catchment area: Britain. Currently two-thirds Scottish, one-third English
Fees: £450 per week. Reviewed every April

Aims to lead adolescents and young adults with severe learning difficulties into maturity through work, crafts and educational/cultural activities.

Courses and facilities

The staff and students are all residential (no separate staff housing); integrated living and working. There is remedial teaching for those who can benefit from it; and teaching by example to achieve social acceptability, personal identity and self reliance. The focus on gardening and craft work, and the active social life, is of help to those who have poor motivation. Students are expected to take an active part in the running of each household, and are encouraged to express their opinions. Templehill has a three term year.

Students accepted: 31 young men and women, all severely disabled, many with multiple disabilities. Site unsuitable for wheelchairs.

Applications/selection: Applications from special education and social services departments. We expect applicants to visit. Criteria for admission are:

- Would applicant be rightly placed socially, and able to integrate with other students?

- Is applicant likely to respond to, and benefit from, our facilities and way of life?

Out-of-term contact: Senior staff always in residence during holidays.

Tulath House

247 Gower Road, Sketty, Swansea SA2 9JL
Tel: 01792 201405
Age range: 16-25
Catchment area: Unrestricted
Controlled by: The Richmond Fellowship
Fees: £706 per week

Tulath House offers residential and day placements for young adults with emotional and behavioural problems and mild learning difficulties. We aim to promote the health, ability and potential of the individual by fostering, within a therapeutic, residential environment, a sense of social responsibility, membership of the community and active participation in the wider society.

General description

A large detached house with a large garden, 10 single bedrooms, large lounge, kitchen, dining room, study, television room, artroom, hallway and office. Outhouses include laundry and kiln room.

Staffing: Multi-disciplinary team including teaching staff, and others from a background of training in psychiatric nursing.

Students accepted: 10 residential students and up to four day students, men and women, recovering mentally ill and/or with mild learning difficulties.

Applications/selection Application forms, information pack and admissions criteria obtainable from Tulath. All relevant reports to accompany application. Residential assessment period essential. Ongoing support from referring social worker or other professional must be maintained throughout the placement.

Courses and facilities

Our education curriculum offers a flexible, activity-based programme designed to develop, through positive reinforcement, educational, personal and social skills. It incorporates a framework for assessment, accredits all achievement and allows progression to recognised courses.

We give recognition to the significance of the Accreditation of Prior Learning and Achievement as a means to planning appropriate levels as well as building on strengths and achievements, thus facilitating a progression route during a student's placement at Tulath and beyond it, into mainstream college courses, open learning colleges, adult continuing education, etc. Integrated core skills. We are committed to equality of opportunity in education and training.

Links with other establishments

Guidance and advice from the Careers Business Company; strong links exist with Swansea College and Adult Continuing Education and all students are encouraged to integrate into some courses outside Tulath; befriending schemes operate and services are strongly supported by committed volunteers; strong links exist with Swansea MIND and the local self advocacy group and students are encouraged to use these services where appropriate; students are encouraged to join clubs and night classes, to pursue hobbies and interests, and to structure their leisure time.

Valence School

Westerham, Kent TN16 1QN
Tel: 01959 562156 Fax: 01959 565046
Principal: Roland Gooding
Age range: 16 + ; 11-16; 5-11
Catchment area: Mainly South East England, but applicants from further afield will be considered.
Controlled by: Kent County Council
Fees: Contact the Special Needs Manager for further details

General description

'A good school striving for excellence' OFSTED July 1997. Valence is situated in 40 acres of parkland, facilities include indoor swimming and hydrotherapy pools, covered sports area, specialist classrooms and therapy accommodation. There are separate primary and post 16 facilities. The school regularly hosts consultant outpatient clinics from the London teaching hospitals. The local authority communication and curriculum access advisor is based with the education team at the school.

Staffing: Specialist qualified teaching staff, physiotherapists, occupational therapists, speech and language therapists, specialist nursing and care teams.

Students accepted: Those with physical disabilities and/or complex medical needs with associated learning, social and/or emotional difficulties. It is important that all students at post 16 are able to independently follow nationally-accredited courses at entry level or above.

Applications/selection: Initially through specialist careers officers and/or local authorities frequently with advice of medical profession.

Courses and facilities

The FE phase is in a separate building with specialist teaching and living facilities, however students are encouraged to play a leading role in arranging and facilitating school activities.

- GNVQ Foundation: business, health and social care, information technology and leisure and tourism.
- GNVQ Intermediate: business, health and social care and information technology.
- GNVQ Advanced: (single awards in consortia with local network schools).
- National Skills Profile and OCR entry level vocational awards (care & office practice).
- Skills for independent living with an emphasis on independent travel, driving (the school has its own fully adapted car for students to learn to drive in), independent cooking and managing personal finances.

Links with other establishments

The FE phase has active links with a range of other schools and colleges in the area and students are encouraged to use the full potential of the local community for educational and recreational purposes.

Out-of-term contact: The school or the Special Needs Manager, West Kent Area Office, 39 Grove Hill Road, Tunbridge Wells, TN1 1SL Tel: 01892 523342.

The West of England College

Countess Wear, Exeter, Devon EX2 6HA
Tel: 01392 454245/01392 454200 Fax: 01392 430517
College Director: Harry Dicks
Age range: 16-19 +
Catchment area: South/South-West England and South Wales
Controlled by: Non-maintained and recognised by DfEE
Fees: Paid by students' home LEAs or FEFC

The College aims to extend the students' academic education; provide vocational and pre-vocational training; develop the students' personal and social competence and promote independence.

General description

The West of England College is purpose-built and caters for 50 blind and partially-sighted students.

The College is a branch of the West of England School for Children with Little or No Sight and has access to the School's excellent facilities. The College is situated away from the main school and functions independently and with its own ethos.

Provision is made for day and boarding students. Boarding is on a termly basis with exeat weekends and half-term breaks. All students are accommodated in single study bedrooms. There is a full weekend leisure programme in which students are encouraged to participate.

Applications/selection: Telephone the West of England College for information and to arrange a visit. Applicants will have an advice and guidance meeting followed by a three-day assessment which is free of charge.

Students accepted: Visually-impaired students, including those with learning difficulties and additional disabilities.

Courses and facilities

The College offers a wide range of academic and vocational courses. Students are included in courses at local colleges for their studies, supported by the specialist staff and resources of the West of England College. Staff are available in the evenings to provide any additional support the students need. The College provides an 'in house' programme for students with additional learning difficulties and disabilities.

On leaving the College, many students obtain employment or are accepted for training schemes; others enter higher education. Full careers guidance is regularly available to all students.

The pastoral aspect of the curriculum is delivered by an experienced team of care staff who work closely with individual students, encouraging them to make their own decisions and take responsibility for themselves. An independence living skills programme, mobility training and an active leisure programme are vital aspects of the extended curriculum offered to all students. The aim is to provide a friendly, supportive and stimulating environment in which students can learn, develop and become as independent as possible.

All students have access to counsellors, including a clinical psychologist and an educational psychologist.

The campus has an excellent medical centre with RGN cover. The ophthalmic surgeon, paediatrician and other specialists visit on a regular basis. Other services include audiology, speech therapy, occupational therapy and physiotherapy. Health education is also provided.

The specialist environment of the West of England College is tailored to respond positively to the needs of the individual and to provide a bridge between school and adult life.

Links with other establishments

Close links with two local colleges: Exeter College and St Loye's College.

Out-of-term contact: Tel: 01392 454200 - the Main School office.

Westwood School

Blithbury, Rugeley, Staffordshire WS15 3JQ
Tel: 01889 504353 Fax: 01889 504361
Website: www.honormead.btinternet.com
Email: westwoodschool@honormead.btinternet.com
Principal: Ms S Hodge
Catchment area: National   Age range: 5-19
Controlled by: Honormead Schools Ltd
Fees: Termly boarding - £14,370; termly day - £8,620;
50 week boarding - £16,920 per term; 52 week boarding -
£17,640 per term (Extra care hours available)

Aims to reflect education, care and language and communication therapy in the whole school curriculum. Presents a safe, happy, stimulating and challenging environment. Provides creative and imaginative teaching through meaningful partnerships between parents, responsible agencies and the school. Promotes the physical, intellectual, cultural, moral and spiritual development of all pupils to meet personal and social goals in the wider community.

General description

Westwood School is situated in rural countryside close to the town of Rugeley near Lichfield in Staffordshire. The school admits pupils with severe learning difficulties which may be associated with the autistic continuum including intentional communication deficit, fine and gross motor problems and behaviour difficulties.

Staffing: Student support assistants, teachers, speech and language therapists, occupational therapists, educational psychologist, riding therapists and other school support staff.

Students accepted: Day and residential placements for pupils with severe learning difficulties which may be associated with the autistic continuum including intentional communication deficit, fine and gross motor problems and behaviour difficulties.

Application/selection: Application through Statement of Special Educational Needs and subject to satisfactory assessment.

Courses and facilities

Access to National Curriculum, assessment and external accreditation and examinations. Academic and vocational education, careers guidance and work experience. Community and work based activities. Enhanced independence and personal responsibility, spiritual, moral and cultural development.

Links with other establishments

Mainstream schools and FE colleges. Parents and local authority professionals, Green Laund, FE centre.

William Morris Camphill Community

Eastington, Stonehouse, Gloucestershire GL10 3SH
Tel/Fax: 01453 824025
Principal: Management Group
Catchment area: Unrestricted   Age range: 16-25
Controlled by: Correspondent
Fees: 1999/2000 £15,688 - £18,231

Aims to continue education and training as a preparation for life. Developing ability, skills and encouraging independence for adult life whether in the community or a sheltered environment.

General description

Began in 1978. A college and training centre in Severn Valley. (Stroud four miles, Stonehouse one mile, Gloucester ten miles). The main house accommodates 17 young people in two separate extended family groups. Two additional houses for eight young people and three independent young people. Large gardens; pottery; weaving; woodwork and food processing workshops. There is also a farm community nearby for older trainees, offering agricultural training.

Staffing: Residential co-workers, teachers and craft workshop instructors, supported by therapists and artists.

Students accepted: Those with learning difficulties, also including social and multiple difficulties.

Applications/selection: Application form and prospectus on request, followed by interview. If applicable, trial visit is arranged. Vacancy situation dictates waiting period. Registered with Gloucestershire Social Services.

Courses and facilities

For those between 16 and 19 we offer a three-year further education course each morning with students receiving a training in a workshop activity in the afternoons. During this time they spend a term (twelve weeks) in each workshop. This offers an opportunity to develop a wide range of craft and skill abilities. At 19, further education continues but the emphasis is on craft training and employability skills. Additionally we offer drama, music, adventure training, horse riding and educational trips.

Links with other establishments

Courses available at Stroud College.

Out-of-term contact: Admissions group.

The Wing Centre, Southlands School

Vicar's Hill, Boldre, Near Lymington, Hants SO41 5QB
Tel: 01590 675350 Fax: 01590 671891
Head (Acting): Mrs Sue Gething, BEd
Catchment area: Nationwide   Age range: 9-16, 16-19
Controlled by: The Hesley Group, The Coach House, Hesley
Hall, Tickhill, Doncaster, South Yorkshire DN11 9HH
Tel: 01302 866906 Fax: 01302 865473
Fees: On request from the Head

COPE

The aim of all Hesley Group schools and colleges is to enable people with special needs to achieve their full potential. The full potential for people with Asperger's Syndrome, who are often of average or above average intelligence, can seem totally elusive some days because of their lack of normal social and communication skills. Southlands and the Wing Centre aim to provide students with sufficient socialising, communication, life and independent living skills to enable them to move on to as normal a life as possible.

General description

Southlands School is a termly boarding school offering supported education and guidance to young men with Asperger's Syndrome and high functioning autism. The Wing Centre is the post-16 department of Southlands School.

Students accepted: 61 termly placements. Students should have a diagnosis of Asperger's Syndrome or high functioning autism. Students are placed and funded by Local Education Authorities, Social Services or Health Departments.

Referrals and admissions: A student cannot be considered for a placement until an official request is received from the LEA, Social Services, or other referring agency. However, parents are encouraged to visit on Parent Open Days on an informal basis so that they can meet the staff and students and feel able to suggest the school as appropriate for their son. Please contact the school for the date of the next open day.

Parent Partnership: The school is a strong advocate of teamwork between all agencies, and especially the student's parents and family. Contact with parents is maintained throughout the student's life at Southlands, through regular phone calls, visits home and visits by parents to the school.

Southlands is an independent special school approved by the DfEE. The campus which houses the primary, secondary and the Post 16 departments is located in the New Forest, near the south coast town of Lymington. The school has its own outdoor swimming pool, angling pond, extensive grounds both wooded and grassed, and a hard-court recreation surface. There is an indoor gym. Southlands is not a secure site: there are few locked doors or gates. Students are trusted to stay on site and abide by the rules and arrangements in place for their safety. Staffing ratios are set at 1:3.

Courses and facilities

Students follow the National Curriculum, which is incorporated in the Southlands "Lifestyles" curriculum. Students with Asperger's Syndrome need time to learn, process, practise, revise, over-learn and generalise skills. The Lifestyles curriculum allows them to develop these skills and adapt to life in what for them can be a confusing world. All students at Southlands will be offered a supportive and therapeutic environment. In the Wing Centre students will be offered courses including ASDAN Youth Awards, City & Guilds Skillpower, RSA CLAIT, and some GCSEs. Some shared provision with local post-16 colleges is available where appropriate.

Links with the community: This is an essential part of the daily life of our students, and includes leisure pursuits – skating, horse-riding, swimming, and bowling – and social training, when they will visit local shops, cafes and, when age appropriate, pubs; learn to use public transport and other amenities.

Work Experience: Several work experience placements will be arranged during a student's time at the Wing Centre. These are always well researched, monitored and evaluated.

Winslow Court

Rowden House School, Winslow, Bromyard,
Herefordshire HR7 4LS
Tel: 01885 488096 Fax: 01885 483361
Residential Manager: Dom Ellsmore
Age range: 20 +
Controlled by: Registered with Hereford & Worcester Social Services

Aims to provide an environment in which residents will be able to achieve their potential capacity - physically, intellectually, emotionally and socially.

General description

A purpose-built facility developed from the original courtyard buildings at Rowden House. The Unit is single-storey and provides 24 single bedrooms. Designed to provide four separate independent units, each having kitchen, dining and recreation facilities. In addition, a communal kitchen, dining room, training rooms and recreational area enable staff to offer social activities to the larger group and individual training and therapies. Transport is provided for shopping, recreation and off-site leisure pursuits.

Staffing: Residential manager, four unit leaders, 42 care staff, waking and sleeping night-time supervision. Medical, dental, physiotherapy and special training input is available from outside agencies.

Students accepted: Severe learning difficulties and behavioural problems.

Courses and facilities

Two occupational therapy rooms provide opportunities for structured activities and training in artwork, woodwork, pottery, weaving and associated crafts. The extensive grounds offer facilities for horticulture and animal husbandry. Local college placements offer further skills-training.

Wirral Autistic Society - Raby Hall Autistic Community

Raby Hall Road, Bromborough, Wirral, Merseyside CH63 0NN
Tel: 0151 334 7150 Fax: 0151 334 1762
Website: www.wirral.autistic.org/
Email: was@wirraut.demon.co.uk
Chief Executive: M J Hatton
Age range: 18 +
Catchment area: Nationwide, although preference will be given to applicants from Wirral
Fees: Presently £658 - £680 per week, fully residential. Day attenders fee: £382 per week. Monday to Friday (dependent on level of care required)

Aims to provide for people with autism, a secure and structured environment with opportunities for those more able clients to develop skills in independent living.

General description

In order to cater for the whole range of abilities throughout the autistic continuum, the Wirral Autistic Society offers accommodation on a variety of sites. Raby Old Hall is a 15-bed Victorian house which offers intensive support for the most highly-dependent residents, with Helen House offering a supervised and structured environment to 16 people who are less dependent. In a nearby village, 'The Green' consists of four self-contained flats for ten more independent people with autism who require minimal support and supervision, and 'The Lodge' caters for people who are able to live independently. The Society also provides a number of 2/3 bedroom houses in the local community, providing independent lifestyle for a number of adults with autism, with the advantage of staff support.

Staffing: Chief executive, deputy chief executive, head of social work, assistant heads of social work, residential social workers, co-workers, head of day services, assistant head of day services, day service officers, maintenance team, finance team, administration team, domestic staff, training & development officer, personnel & training officer, outreach/family support worker, appeals officer, community support manager. Total staff complement 180.

Clients accepted: Only those people who have been diagnosed as autistic or Asperger's Syndrome, usually over 18 years old, male or female.

Applications/selection: Interested applicants are invited to pay a visit to the Society, to view the facilities. Application forms are available from the secretary. When completed, these are held until a suitable vacancy becomes available.

Courses and facilities

Day services are offered in a separate industrial therapy unit, offering training in: outdoor pursuits; horticulture; woodwork & furniture restoration; pottery; printing; silkscreen printing; domestic/social skills; PE; further education; music; speech therapy; computer skills.

A swimming pool and gymnasium are available on-site, and work experience is offered in the Raby Hall Garden Centre.

Links with other establishments

The Wirral Autistic Society is an autonomous organisation, affiliated to and accredited by the National Autistic Society, and other autistic societies throughout the UK.

Out-of-term contact: Raby Hall is open 365 days a year. There are staff available 24 hours a day.

Woodlarks Workshop Trust

Lodge Hill Road, Farnham, Surrey GU10 3RB
Tel: 01252 714041
Chairman: Mr S G Farrant
Catchment area: Countrywide   Age range: 18 +
Controlled by: Management Committee
Fees: £283.50 per week

Aims to achieve maximum independence within the disability in a secure and happy home environment.

General description

An independently run home and sheltered workshop for 21 physically disabled adults. Workshop activities include a wide variety of handcrafts.

Staffing: Joint Managers - administrator/head of care; one full-time and six part-time senior care staff; one full-time and one part-time junior care staff; one full-time and two part-time cooks, one full-time workshop supervisor and four workshop volunteers (part-time); one groundsman and contract cleaners.

Students accepted: Adults.

Applications/selection All applications considered to conform with residential home standards.

Courses and facilities

Residents are encouraged to participate in Adult Education courses, and social activities etc within the community.

Links with other establishments

Member of Surrey Registered Homes Association.

Yateley Industries for the Disabled

Mill Lane, Yateley, Hants GU46 7TF
Tel: 01252 872337 Fax: 01252 860620
General Manager Mrs L Robinson
Age range: 16-65
Catchment area: Nationwide
Controlled by: Council of Management

Aims to enhance the lives of disabled people by providing remunerative employment and warden-assisted accommodation.

General description

Self-contained custom-built village - three acres in centre of Yateley - producing hand and screen printed textiles for sale. Hostel and bungalows for residents are grouped around a pleasant lawn, and the workshop is situated nearby. Within wheeling distance of most shops; own welfare bus provides transport to swimming lessons and classes of further education.

Staffing: General Manager, Production Manager, Care Manager, Finance Officer; sales assistant; two wardens; two part-time canteen staff; controllers and workshop supervisory staff.

Students accepted: Must have use of upper limbs and have the potential to live independently, with sufficient mental ability to live and work with minimal supervision. No other restrictions on ability. Cannot accept those with blindness or those requiring nursing care.

Applications/selection: Visits are welcomed. Apply direct or through DEA or social worker. Waiting period for assessment is dependent on the applicant's county social services department being willing to fund the cost and to give financial support when the applicant becomes an employee. Full training is provided.

Courses and facilities

Assessment for suitability for employment in hand block or screen printing, and machine sewing. Living skills will also be assessed. Four weeks duration. Intakes throughout the year.

Work and domestic training provided. The aim is to provide an environment in which the individual can realise his/her full potential. Up to four people live in self-sustaining groups, and work in similar groups, each under its own disabled leader. Support is always available, but unobtrusive, and increasingly withdrawn as independence grows. Employment is offered to those willing to undertake the work and who can make a significant contribution to production.

Links with other establishments

Other supported workshops and Yateley centre for adult literacy.

COPE

Index of Establishments by Location

London, South East and East Anglia

(Bedfordshire, Cambridgeshire, East Sussex, Essex, Hertfordshire, Kent, London, Norfolk, Suffolk, Surrey and West Sussex)

South and South West

(Berkshire, Buckinghamshire, Cornwall, Devon, Dorset, Gloucestershire, Hampshire, Isle of Wight, Oxfordshire, Somerset, Wiltshire)

Apsley House

Beddington Centre

Catherine House

Cherry Orchards (Camphill Community) Ltd

Cintre Community

Dame Hannah Rogers School

Enham Trust

Fairfield Opportunity Farm (Dilton) Ltd

Farleigh College

Fortune Centre of Riding Therapy

George House

Grange Village Community

Grenville College

The Hatch (Camphill Community)

Ivers

Living Options

The Loddon School

Lord Mayor Treloar College

Lufton Manor College

MacIntyre Care

Mary Hare Grammar School for the Deaf

Minstead Training Project

The National Society for Epilepsy Chalfont Centre

National Star Centre College of Further Education

Oaklands Park Village Community

Oakwood Court

Peredur Farm and Craft Centre

Peredur Garden and Craft Centre

Philip Green Memorial School

RNIB Manor House

RNID Poolemead Centre

Royal West of England College for the Deaf

Ruskin Mill Further Education Centre

St Catherine's School

St Christopher's School

St Joseph's Extended Education Unit

St Loye's (Assessment & Development Centre)

SCOPE Thorngrove Centre

Sheiling Community

Somerset Court

Stroud Court

Taurus Crafts

The West of England College

William Morris (Camphill Community)

Wing Centre, Southlands School

Midlands

(Derbyshire, Hereford and Worcester, Leicestershire, Lincolnshire, Northamptonshire, Nottinghamshire, Shropshire, Staffordshire, Warwickshire, West Midlands)

Alderwasley Hall School

Bladon House School

Broughton House College

Cottage and Rural Enterprises Ltd (CARE)

Derby College for Deaf People

Derwen College for the Disabled

Exhall Grange School

Grange Vocational Assessment and Training Centre

Hereward College of Further Education

Hinwick Hall College of Further Education

Homefield College of FE and Vocational Training

Honormead School for Children with Autism

Landmarks

Longdon Hall School

Loppington House

Overley Hall School

Portland College for People with Disabilities

Queen Alexandra College of Further Education

RNIB Condover Hall School

RNIB New College

RNIB Vocational College

Robinia Advantage

Royal National College for the Blind

SENSE West

Solden Hill House

Strathmore House

Westwood School

Winslow Court

North

(Cheshire, Cumbria, Durham, Greater Manchester, Lancashire, Merseyside, Northumberland, Tyne and Wear, Yorkshire)

Beaumont College of Further Education

Birtenshaw Hall School

Botton Village

Boys and Girls Welfare Society

Croft Community

David Lewis Organisation

Deafway (formerly the Mary Cross Trust)

165

Dilston College

Doncaster College for the Deaf

Finchale Training College

Fourways Assessment Unit

Henshaw's College

Hesley Village College

Holly Bank School

Home Farm Trust

Larchfield Community

Lindeth College

Northern Counties School for the Deaf

Nugent House School

Pennine Camphill Community

Royal Schools for the Deaf, Manchester

Weelsby Hall Further Education College

Wirral Autistic Society Raby Hall Community

Wales

Bryn Melyn

Coleg Elidyr

Furze Mount

Mental Health Care Group

Pengwern College

St David's Care in the Community

Tulath

Scotland

Beannacher

Camphill Blair Drummond

Camphill Rudolf Steiner Schools

Corseford School for Spastics

Easter Anguston Training Farm

Garvald

Garvald Centre

Motherwell College

RNIB Alwyn House

Templehill Community (Camphill)

Index of Establishments by Disabilities and Disorders

This index has been compiled from information provided by the establishments themselves, and entries have been made where they have expressed a particular interest or expertise in a specific disability or range of disabilities. It is by no means an exhaustive list, and further study of individual entries is advised.

The following categories are used:

Autism/Asperger's Syndrome

Blindness/visual disabilities

Blind/deaf – visual/hearing impaired

Cerebral palsy

Deafness/hearing impairment

Disadvantage

Dyslexia

Emotional disorders/maladjustment

Epilepsy

Learning difficulties/disabilities

Mental Health

Mixed and multiple disabilities

Physical disabilities

Speech impairment

Autism/ Asperger's Syndrome

Alderwasley Hall School

Boys & Girls Welfare Society

Broughton Hall School

Catherine House

Farleigh College

The Helen Allison School

Hesley Village College

Homefield College of FE and Vocational Training

Honormead School for Children with Autism

Linkage Specialist Further Education College

The Loddon School

Longdon Hall School

The Lothlorien Community

MacIntyre Care

Overley Hall School

Philpots Manor School & Further Training Course

Queen Alexander College of Further Education

Royal Schools for the Deaf Manchester

Ruskin Mill Further Education Centre

St John's College

Somerset Court

Stroud Court

Westwood School

Wing Centre, Southlands School

Wirral Autistic Society Raby Hall Community

Blindness/visual disabilities

Dorton College of Further Education

Exhall Grange School

Henshaw's College

Hereward College

Linkage Specialist College

Motherwell College

Queen Alexandra College of Further Education

RNIB Alwyn House

RNIB Condover Hall School

RNIB Manor House

RNIB New College

RNIB Redhill College

RNIB Vocational College

Royal National College for the Blind

St Joseph's Extended Educational Unit

seeAbility

SENSE East

SENSE West

The West of England College

Blind/deaf visual/hearing impaired

Linkage Specialist College

Lord Mayor Treloar College

Queen Alexander College of FE

RNIB Condover Hall School

SENSE East

SENSE West

Cerebral palsy (see also physical disabilities)

Beaumont College of Further Education

Birtenshaw Hall School

Corseford School for Spastics

Hereward College of Further Education

Linkage Specialist College

SCOPE Thorngrove Centre

Communication/ language/speech impairment

Alderwasley Hall School

Bladon House School

Dame Hannah Rogers School

Hereward College

Linkage Specilist College

Longdon Hall School

Lufton Manor College

MacIntyre Care

Motherwell College

Philip Green Memorial School

Pield Heath House RC School

Royal Schools for the Deaf, Manchester

St Catherine's School

St John's College

St Joseph's School

Deafness/ hearing impairment

Deafway

Derby College for Deaf People

Doncaster College for the Deaf

Linkage Specialist College

Mary Hare Grammar School for the Deaf

Northern Counties School for the Deaf

Ovingdean Hall School

RNID Poolemead Centre

Royal Schools for the Deaf, Manchester

Royal School for Deaf Children and Westgate College

Royal West of England College for the Deaf

Disadvantage

Bryn Melyn

George House

Dyslexia

Grenville College

Linkage Specialist College

Queen Alexander College of Further Education

Emotional disorders/ maladjustment

Allington Manor School & Therapeutic Community

Apsley House

Boys & Girls Welfare Society

Bryn Melyn

Camelia Botnar Foundation

Cintre Community

Delrow College

Fortune Centre of Riding Therapy

The Hatch (Camphill Community)

Homefield College of Further Education & Vocational Training

Ivers

Jaques Hall Foundation

Linkage Specialist College

Loppington House

The Mount Camphill Community

Nugent House School

Pennine Camphill Community

Peredur Farm and Craft Centre

Peredur Garden and Craft Centre

Philpots Manor School and Further Training Course

Robinia Advantage

Ruskin Mill Further Education Centre

Tulath House

Valence School

Westwood School

William Morris (Camphill Community)

Winslow Court

Epilepsy

David Lewis Organisation

Ivers

Linkage Specialist College

MacIntyre Care

The National Society for Epilepsy

Philpots Manor School and Further Education Training Course

St Elizabeth's School

St John's College

St Piers

Learning difficulties/ disabilities

Acorn Village

Apsley Trust

Beannacher

Beaumont College of Further Education

Beddington Centre

Blandon House School

Botton Village

Britenshaw Hall School

Broughton House College

Camphill Blair Drummond

CAmphill Rudolf Steiner Schools

Cintre Community

Coleg Elidyr

Cottage & Rural Enterprises Ltd

Croft Community

Dame Hannah Rogers School

David Lewis Organisation

Delrow College

Derwen Collage for the Disabled

Dilston College

Easter Anguston Training Farm

Enham Trust

Fairfield Opportunity Farm

Fortune Centre of Riding Therapy

Furze Mount

Garvald - West Linton

Garvald Centre - Edinburgh

Grange Centre for People with Disabilities

Grange Village Community

Grenville College

Hatch (Camphill Community)

Hereward College of Further Education

Hesley Village College

Holly Bank School

Home Farm Trust

Homefield College of Further Education & Vocational Training

Ivers

Landmarks

Larchfield Community

Lindeth college

Linkage Specialist College

Loddon School

Longdon Hall School

Loppington House

Lufton Manor College

MacIntyre

Meldreth Manor School

Mental Health Care Group

Minstead Training Project

Motherwell College

Nash Further Education Centre

Nexus Direct Programme

Oakland Village Community

Oakwood Court

Overley Hall School

Papworth Trust

Pengwern College

Pennine Camphill Community

Philip Green Memorial School

Pield Heath House RC School

Ruskin Mill Further Education Centre

St Christopher's School

St David's Care in the Community

St Elizabeth's School

St John's College

St Joseph's School

Searchlight Workshops

Sheiling Community

Solden Hill House

Strathmore House

Taurus Crafts

Templehill Community (Camphill)

Tulath House

Westwood School

William Morris (Camphill Community)

Winslow Court

Mental health problems

Cherry Orchards (Camphill Community) Ltd

Furze Mount

Mental Health Care Group

Nugent House School

Pennine Camphill Community

Searchligh Workshops

Taurus Crafts

Mixed and multiple disabilities

Alderwasley Hall School

Birtenshaw Hall School

Broughton House College

Camphill Rudolf Steiner Schools

Exhall Grange School

Finchale Training College

Fortune Centre of Riding Therapy

Fourways Assessment Unit

Hereward College

Hinwick Hall College of Further Education

Homefield College of Further Education and Vocational Training

Ivers

Linkage Specialist College

Loddon School

Lothlorien Community

MacIntyre Care

Motherwell College

Mount Camphill Community

Northern Counites School for the Deaf

Overley Hall School

Pennine Camphill Community

Queen Alexander College of Further Education

RNIB Manor House

Royal National College for the Blind (RNC)

Royal Schools for the Deaf Manchester

Ruskin Mill Further Education Centre

St David's Care in the Community

St Elizabeth's School

St John's College

St Joseph's Extended Education Unit

St Joseph's School

Searchlights Workshops

Taurus Crafts

Temphill Community

West of England College

**Physical
disabilities**

Banstead Place Brain Injury Rehabilitation Centre

Beddington Centre

Birtenshaw Hall School

Boys & Girls Welfare Society

Bridget's Hostel for Students with Disabilities

Dame Hannah Rogers School

Dorincourt

Enham Trust

Finchdale Training College

Fortune Centre of Riding Therapy

Foursways Assessment Unit

The Grange Centre for People with Disabilities

Hereward College

Hinwick Hall College of Further Education

Holly Bank School

Landmarks

Lindeth college

Linkage Specialist College

Living Options

Lord Mayor Treloar College

The Lothlorien Community

Love Walk

Meldreth Manor School

Motherwell College

Nash House Further Education Centre

National Star Centre College of Further Education

Orpheus Centre

The Papworth Trust

Portland College for People with Disabilities

Queen Elizabeth's Training College

RNID Poolemead

St Davids Care in the Community

St Joseph's Extended Education Unit

St Loye's (Initial Training Centre)

St Piers

Searchlight Workshops

Taurus Crafts

Toynton Hall Further Education College

Valence School

Weelsby Hall Further Education College

Woodlarks Workshop Trust

Yateley Industries for the Disabled Ltd

Index

I

J

L

M

N

O

T

V

W

Y